'There is no present like your future.'
Adrian Beale

Presented to:

_____

From:

_____

Date:

_____

The *Mystic* Awakening

Revealing the Ancient Secrets of God's Seers

Adrian Beale

DESTINY IMAGE® PUBLISHERS, INC.
P.O. Box 310, Shippensburg, PA
17257-0310
"Promoting Inspired Lives."

This book and all other Destiny Image, Revival Press, MercyPlace, Fresh Bread, Destiny Image Fiction, and Treasure House books are available at Christian bookstores and distributors worldwide.

For a U.S. bookstore nearest you, call 1-800-722-6774.

For more information on foreign distributors, call 717-532-3040. Reach us on the Internet: www.destinyimage.com.

ISBN 13 TP: 978-0-7684-0418-0
ISBN 13 Ebook: 978-0-7684-0419-7

For Worldwide Distribution, Printed in the U.S.A.

3 4 5 6 7 8 / 18 17 16

Dedication

This book is dedicated to my beloved wife Lesley, without whose love, understanding and patience this book would not exist.

Acknowledgments

Special thanks to Rhonda Pooley and my daughter Rebekah Beale. To Rhonda for proofreading and correcting the original manuscript and to Bek for typesetting, and designing the layout, and illustrating the final document.

Thanks to all my friends and the unnamed encouragers whose lives and words have contributed to this book.

Rhonda Pooley - copyediting, proofreading, ghostwriting
rhonte@gmail.com

Rebekah Beale - graphic design, website, cover photography.
www.bekbee.com

Key to Annotations

cf. compare
eg. for example
f. verse or page that follows
ff. verses or pages following
ie. that is
NB. Note well
NT. New Testament
OT. Old Testament
Selah. pause and meditate on that

(G 770) Strong's Greek Concordance number
(H1545) Strong's Hebrew Concordance number
(f) Sidenote found in side column
(3) Scripture reference found in footnotes.
(A) Bibliography reference found at end of chapter.

This book is meant to be read, digested, highlighted, underlined and your own notes added to the side columns as the Holy Spirit uses the content as a catalyst to reveal His personal words of revelation to you.

Contents

Tables & Diagrams

Endorsements

We are at a place in church history where there is a deep hunger for the God who answers by fire. There is a rising Glory Generation that are not satisfied with the status quo but are looking to see and experience the living God in ways not yet experienced. The Apostle Paul called Jesus the "Great Mystic Secret of God" where all supernatural knowledge is laid up and stored. We've been given access into God's treasure room to bring forth and manifest those riches on the earth. Adrian Beale has done an amazing job in his new book *The Mystic Awakening* in bringing these truths to light. In this book you will discover truths to unlocking the Supernatural Kingdom of heaven in your life. I highly recommend this book to all that are hungry and thirsty for more!!

Jeff Jansen
Senior Leader
Global Fire Church & Global Connect
Global Fire Ministries International
Kingdom Life Institute & Global Fire School of Supernatural Ministry

There are many "dessert-books" being released these days; books that are sweet, comforting and taste good, but provide no real nutritional value. *The Mystic Awakening*, however, is like a full course dinner that's not only appetizing, but also something you can really sink your teeth into. By a Spirit of Revelation, author Adrian Beale, unlocks the Word of God in a way that will propel you into a Kingdom lifestyle of power and purpose that all flows out of the presence of God and your divine union with Christ. *The Mystic Awakening* is a present-day textbook for releasing heaven on earth through understanding the poetic and parabolic language of the Spirit of God through dreams, visions and the revelatory realm. This is a book no Bible College or ministry school should be without.

Eric D. Green
Co-Founder & Overseer
Global Fire School of Supernatural Ministry
Kingdom Life Institute
www.ericgreen.org

I loved Adrian Beale's book *The Mystical Awakening*. The great reformation of 1514 was just the beginning of God's plan to restore all things. In some ways the reformation dismissed the mystical elements of the Church and much truth has been veiled, however a new reformation is upon us. *The Mystical Awakening* is a book that will bring understanding to the mystical from a biblical perspective. I highly recommend this book to all seekers of truth and reformation. This book has the potential to spark a release of heaven in the earth that will bring revolution in the thinking of the Sons of God.

Ian Johnson
His Amazing Glory Ministries
Auckland - New Zealand
www.hisamazinggloryministries.org

There are a lot of books out there offered to the body of Christ, and yet we only have so much time to spend reading. That is why I STRONGLY suggest this book, *The Mystic Awakening*. As you read you will find revelation opening up, calling to the 'deep unto deep' within you. Your heart will be strengthened and encouraged as the bigger picture in God's heart unfolds in the pages of this book. We have been created for this unprecedented hour of the merging of Heaven and Earth, but have lacked understanding as to the role we are to play as we join the ones who have gone before us in the culmination and restoration of Heaven on the earth. Grounded in the Word and well researched in the Hebrew language, Adrian presents to us an invitation to the true nature of the call of the mystic in all of us as we pursue the heart and desire of God. Thank you, Adrian, for all of your time and effort poured out and your yielded heart to the Spirit of God in the unfolding of this scroll in the earth. It's not just another book.

JoAnn McFatter
Worship leader and speaker
joannmcfatter.com

We love this book. I'm pretty sure it was also on my destiny scroll, but Adrian seems to have got to it first! Bless him for his diligence in putting into simple language, backed up with scripture, God's calling to His favourite creation, Mankind, to delve deeper into the mysteries of the Almighty, the Kingdom, the Heavens and the Supernatural way of life which God had originally intended for us all. I love how easy it is to navigate through the topics and how Adrian breaks it down into bite-size morsels to chew on and digest one at a time as the reader is lead into this amazing feast which the Father has laid for all the Church to partake. Thanks, Adrian, for giving this book to the Bride of Christ, to encourage us all into the supernatural lifestyle of asking, seeking, and finding Him.

Matt and Pearl Nagy
Glory Company, UK

Amidst clear research and deeper explanation of some familiar stories and passages, there lies much treasure that we have been blessed to discover within Adrian's writing. It is refreshing to read of the emphases given along with explanations as to why we need to return to the foundations of our faith; including some often-overlooked cultural and historical nuances that must be revisited. Good meat is something that is chewed thoroughly and savored rather than simply bitten off and swallowed whole, expecting instant satisfaction by mere consumption. *The Mystic Awakening* is a meaty read, yet is easily digested as our appetizer of waiting in God's presence sets the stage and readies us to receive the revelations contained within.

Gary Brooks
Co-founder
In His Image Ministries
www.GaryAndLynn.org

Candy that pops in your mouth comes to mind after reading *The Mystic Awakening* by Adrian Beale. Adrian's work is utterly God inspired. It's obvious he has partnered with the Holy Spirit in producing this exciting book! The mysteries of Heaven unravel as you page through this powerful book. A must read, revealing the ancient paths in today's world!

Veronica Kilrain
Empowering Grace Ministries
allthingsarepossible.com.au

Introduction

One day while in prayer a newly ordained Baptist minister received a vision. In the vision he found himself in a hospital room looking at an Afro-American man who had been hit by a car. The incident had left the man with several broken bones and severe internal organ damage. His injuries were so bad that his heart and lungs were in danger of being pierced by the broken bones in his chest.

In the vision he found himself standing on one side of the bed looking at the man and having an awareness of the complete state of his injuries. Two people came into the room and stood on the other side of the bed. At this point he found himself declaring the man healed. The man leaped from his bed, dressed and discharged himself from the hospital.

A few days later, the patient was found, in a local hospital with the exact conditions as shown in the vision. The visionary and a friend went to the hospital. He described the patient and his clothing in detail and asked his companion to wait at the door to witness what was going to happen.

On entering the hospital he found the room just has he had seen in the vision. He entered and stood exactly where he had seen himself positioned. He waited for the two people to come into the room for the scene to be fulfilled, the patient's wife began to describe her husband's condition and the impossibility of his situation due to the dire nature of his injuries.

Sure enough, the two people came into the room and stood on the other side of the bed. They happened to be the ones who had accidentally ran over the man. When the scene was fully as he had seen it, the visionary declared the man healed. As he did, the man immediately threw back the covers and jumped out of bed, apparently completely healed.

The medical staff, were understandably frantic to restrain the accident victim. However, it was all to no avail, as the man was completely healed. He put on the clothes he had been seen wearing in the vision and vacated the hospital past the visionary's friend at the front door.

This is just a single event documented in the life of one of the past great men of faith. As extraordinary as this may appear, this is just normal everyday behaviour for the sons of God. Right now, all over the world men and women are similarly hearing from God and being used as portals of heaven. A woman in Africa regularly receives guidance about a certain man or woman in a village who will be healed. When she acts on that deposit from God the recipient of healing becomes a catalyst for the rest of the village to be saved. Meanwhile in Australia, a friend of mine waits upon God on his bed and receives visions of people and their physical conditions so that he can bring heaven's intervention to their situation. Similarly, a housewife has a dream that, when interpreted, warns the couple that without intervention their financial investment is in jeopardy. A mum dreams that her married daughter is pregnant and phones her that day to check on her welfare and averts an abortion scheduled for the very next day. This is normal Christianity.

Unfortunately, many of us are settling for much less, having been groomed into something other than the dynamic partnership God intended for every believer who wants to see heaven invade earth. Based on scripture, this book explains and provides insights for developing that partnership and increasing our sensitivity to the voice of the Spirit of God. It also opens unseen layers in the word of God to reveal and map the Ancient Paths - from cover to cover of the Bible - so that believers can see and understand the path ahead and successfully make the journey.

The depth and density of revelation it contains require the reader to take time in digesting its morsels. This is not a book to be rushed. It is designed to be studied, underlined, highlighted and meditated upon, adding your own notes to the side columns.

There is no present like your future
Adrian Beale

Chapter 1

Back to the Future

'Behold, I will send you Elijah the prophet
Before the coming of the great and dreadful day of the LORD
And he will turn the hearts of the fathers to the children,
And the hearts of the children to their fathers....'

—Malachi 4:5-6

Deja vu

On a number of occasions people have asked me, 'How do you understand, "Deja vu" (day-zhar-voo) in the light of our Christian faith?' To which I normally reply, 'Although the term is used more by unbelievers, it does not pose a problem to Christians, in fact, as believers, we should have a better appreciation of it!' Deja vu can be defined as looking at an unfamiliar situation and feeling like you've seen it before. As

1

believers we know that we are first and foremost spiritual beings; spiritual beings not bound by these earthly bodies that house us. It should come as no surprise then that on occasion we may walk into a strange environment having already been there in the Spirit. Our spirit is always active in that other dimension but especially when we forego our earthly agenda and bring focus to seeking and waiting upon God. Another place where we experience excursions into the spirit realm is when we are asleep. It is a revelation to some that dreams and visions of the night are not the result of a busy lifestyle, but that they are, in fact, interactions in the spirit realm; interactions that, to Christians, reveal aspects of the kingdom. Now, dependent on the nature of what is communicated during these glimpses of eternity (that which is outside time) it is not unreasonable to appreciate that some may fall into the category of Deja vu as previews of some pending earthly experience.

As interesting as Deja vu may be for discussion, I believe, in the plan of God, the flip side of the subject is more important. The opposite of Deju vu can legitimately be coined, 'Vuja de' (voo-zhar-day). Believe it or not this is not a new term, it is used in the sporting and business worlds where it is applied to reassess the relevance of current practices and values. Vuja de can be understood as looking at a current and familiar situation through new eyes and asking how did we get here? Effectively, it is looking at the past to get a new line of sight for the future and is of particular interest where there has been gradual change over extended periods of time. The reality is that it is possible for both organizations and individuals to morph into entities that are far from or even diametrically opposed to, their original core values and practices. For example, universities and hospitals which were initially founded on Christian principles are not only void of God in their governance, but have often become the seedbeds of unbelief.

Swiss Watch Industry

The Swiss watch industry, which at one time was used by every change-management advocate as the classic example of an industry incapable of changing with its market, has in recent times made a remarkable recovery. What was once an industry outpaced by quartz technology (which it had pioneered), has once again become the world's market leader.

At the completion of the Second World War the Swiss held 80 percent of the world's watch market. By 1970, with the introduction of quartz technology, the Swiss share of the market was down to 42 percent and by the early 80's the industry was on its last legs. However, rather than embracing the commonly held practice of importing 'off-the-shelf' strategies devised by outside experts, Nicolas G. Hayek, the architect of the Swiss resurgence drew from Switzerland's 450-year history of watchmaking to re-invent the industry. Brands like Omega, Breguet, Longines and Rado have reemerged as market leaders not because they applied modern management's outsourcing or niche-marketing ploys, but by reminding the bankers, executives, employees and customers what their brands were founded upon, what made them distinctive, and by building a game plan around these enduring core values. Hayek, who took the helm of an industry divided and in tatters is quoted as saying, 'We gave Omega its message back' (A). The Swatch Group of companies which he led, has seen the re-invention of an industry that witnessed sales of 5 billion dollars in 2009, employed 26,000 people and experienced profits of $720 million! Please do not misunderstand me, this is not a book about business finance. These figures are included only to confirm this comeback story.

In a somewhat quirky parallel, is it possible that our propensity to emulate those on the so called, 'cutting edge', or following those who appear to be leading change, could bring us to the point where we corporately and individually are potentially adrift from core foundational truths and practices that once marked believers as people of 'the way' (1)? Whatever the verdict, healthy retrospection (the act of looking back) is an investment that can create clarity and confidence to usher in the future. The past can be an unrivalled source of revelation and strength. In rediscovering our path to the present we may find behavioural patterns and customs that need to be dropped, and rediscover virtues and practices that will unlock our future!

The Spirit of Elijah

Jesus revealed that John the Baptist was endued with the spirit of Elijah (2), but there is, in the Book of Malachi a declaration of a mandate upon a corporate Elijah to be released before Christ's second coming,

'And he shall turn the heart of the fathers to the children, and the heart of the children to their fathers....'

Malachi 4:6 (KJV)

This verse can be understood on many levels. Whilst it can legitimately be understood on a literal level as a twofold desire to reunite within families, on a much deeper level it speaks of those mature in the faith (fathers) becoming humble like children (3), and further declares that the 'children' of God, are to take on the heart of the patriarchal and apostolic fathers (4). Carrying this further, 'children' quoted above is the Hebrew word, 'Ben', which is more accurately translated 'Sons'. So, given that there is at this time a worldwide air of expectancy for the revealing of the sons of God (5); the above verse also points to the fact that there has to be an accompanying revealing of true fathers that precedes that event (as fathers beget sons) (a).

(a) 'Fathers' is not a gender specific title. Father refers to those mature in the faith and is better defined as those willing to lay their lives down for those they are nurturing.

(1) Acts 9:2; 18:25; 19:9, 23; 22:4; 24:14. (2) Matthew 11:14. (3) Matthew 18:4. (4) John 8:39. (5) Romans 8:19.

The Ancient Paths

This book is a Vuja de. It is a call to explore the way of those who have gone before us and to prune the overgrowth of cultural and religious packaging which smother spiritual growth. This is the time to rediscover the 'ancient paths' of our faith, for in trekking these ancient paths we will realize that fathers are made. The way forward is actually behind us.

The prophet Jeremiah twice refers to God's people straying from the 'ancient' paths (1). The word 'ancient' is the Hebrew word, 'Olam', and is elsewhere translated, 'Everlasting' and 'Eternal'. Thus, a call to the ancient paths is first a reference to a path that brings us before God (Who inhabits Eternity) (2) and is also an invite to follow in the footsteps of our forefathers who walked that path with God (Enoch, Noah, Abraham, Moses, Elijah, Elisha and David).

Though King David is renowned amongst men as the sweet Psalmist of Israel (3), before God he is more highly prized as the man after His own heart (4). Preachers at one time or another broach the subject of what it was that David did to strengthen himself in the LORD (5). Most assume he worshipped in song, while others suggest he remembered the promises of God. He probably did both. However, I believe the key to what David did is not so much what he did in this realm, but what he did before God! Berkeley translates the phrase, *'a man after God's own heart'*, as, *'a man in harmony with Him'* (B). What is meant is that the two - God and David - are one Spirit. David, by definition, is a mystic. His union in the Spirit is the goal of all Hebrew mystics and is the source and bedrock of his strength. If you are feeling a little uncomfortable about the use of the word, 'Mystic', then please read on.

(1) Jeremiah 6:16; 18:15. (2) Isaiah 57:15. (3) 2 Samuel 23:1. (4) 1 Samuel 13:14; Acts 13:22. (5) 1 Samuel 30:6.

Mystic Roots

Did you know that John's Gospel is the Mystic Gospel? Mysticism can be defined as the quest to experience the presence of God directly. It is the desire to 'see' the invisible God and its goal is to become One with the infinite God. In this pursuit, both seeing and hearing are integrally entwined in experiencing God within the heart or imagination of the visionary. Traditional Jewish mystics hold that the bursting forth of God's glory coincides with the revelation of His name. There are certain Jewish schools of mysticism that believe the Torah (the Law) is the incarnate form of the Divine presence and that the Scriptures contain two layers of meaning, the exoteric (public) and the esoteric (hidden) (b). As proof of this they quote King David,

'Open my eyes that I may perceive the wonders of Your Torah'

Psalm 119:18 (Tanakh translation)

and King Solomon,

'A word fitly spoken is like apples of gold in settings of silver.'

Proverbs 25:11

This group believes that just as a casual observer will not notice the detailed gold encased within the silver setting, so most who browse the Scriptures will not discover the treasure hidden within. Some schools of mysticism believe that this double-layer phenomenon within Scripture applies to all Scripture, while others see it applying to only those Scriptures where the literal meaning appears to contradict natural reason. Finally, there are schools of Hebrew mystics who see every unit within the text as significant, including the individual letters. On this point I am reminded of Jesus saying,

(b) Mystic Tenets:

(1) See the invisible God

(2) Become one with God

(3) Word become incarnate

(4) Layers within scripture

(5) The Hebrew letters themselves individually and in their composite arrangement convey meaning.

6

'For assuredly, I say to you, till heaven and earth pass away, one jot or one tittle shall in no way pass from the law till all is fulfilled.'

Matthew 5:18

And the Jews marvelling after a bout of Jesus teaching in the temple, saying,

'How does this Man know letters, having never studied?'

John 7:15

It should be evident even from a brief introduction to mysticism that John employs concepts in his presentation of Christ's life that tell us that both he and Christ were true mystics (c), as were Noah, Abraham, Moses, Elijah, Elisha and all the prominent men and women of God before them. John opens his Gospel with the incarnation of the Word (1), and continues to reveal Christ as the Light of the world (2). His is the Gospel record that highlights the signs that reveal His glory (3) and which records Jesus saying, *'I and My Father are One'* (4). He points to the fruit of true mystical union when he reports Jesus' declaration, *'I speak that which I have seen with My Father'* (5) and,

'Truly, truly, I say unto you, The Son can do nothing of Himself, but what He sees the Father do: for whatever He does, these also does the Son likewise.'

John 5:19 (KJV Modernized)

John records Jesus speaking *'a word fitly spoken'* when He says, *'Destroy this temple, and in three days I will raise it up'* (6). This was most certainly spoken on another level of understanding than how it was literally received. John's Gospel is recognized as that which portrays Christ as the Divine Eagle,

(c) False Mystics: Unfortunately, many people with a spiritual sensitivity have by-passed the church as irrelevant and powerless and sought expression and development of their gifting in Eastern and New Age mystic schools. Many psychics and clairvoyants are simply 'Seer' prophets who have embraced false teaching because of the churches' abdication of the supernatural. However, they are a counterfeit of the real thing, using occult methods to enter the eternal realms. Any teaching that does not recognize the incarnation of Christ and the worth of His shed blood as the only door to enter the heavenlies is antichrist*. Rather than bringing true mysticism into question, the fact that a counterfeit exists endorses the fact that the genuine exists. The devil has muddied the waters to bring confusion at the critical point of 'liftoff'.

* The word 'antichrist' (Greek: Antichristos) can mean either 'against' Christ or 'instead' of Christ, as a counterfeit.

(1) John 1:1,14. (2) John 8:12. (3) John 2:11. (4) John 10:30. (5) John 8:38. (6) John 2:19.

about which Isaiah aptly tells us,

'But they that wait upon the Lord shall renew their strength;
they shall mount up with wings as eagles....'

Isaiah 40:31 (KJV)

John is the only Gospel writer who records Jesus praying that we would be one with the Father just as He was one with the Father and that the very reason for His prayer is that the world would believe our testimony of Jesus (1).

'That they all may be one; as You, Father, are in Me, and I in You,
that they also may be one in Us: that the world may believe that
You sent Me.'

John 17:21

It is evident that mystical oneness was not simply an Old Testament phenomenon but is the essential foundation for the world to come to belief!

And finally, Jesus' mystical practices are on display as we see Him ascending the mountain to wait in the Father's presence after the feeding of the five thousand (2). We see that He was in this place when He had a vision of Nathaniel under the fig tree (3); when He received Divine instruction to go through Samaria to meet a woman at Jacob's well (4). And that Judas knew he would find Jesus in Gethsemane because Jesus was in the habit of meeting the Father there (5).

Please don't misunderstand me, I am not saying that Jesus was merely a mystic. He is both Son of God and Son of Man. However, as the Son of Man, in choosing not to utilize His Deity, He models for us the mature believer, who lives in mystical union with God. In the writings of Isaiah we hear Jesus

(1) John 17:21. (2) John 6:15. (3) John 1:50. (4) John 4:4 ff. (5) John 18:2.

Himself telling us of His mystical relationship with the Father,

'The Lord God has given Me
the tongue of the learned,
that I should know how to speak
a word in season to him that is weary:
He wakens morning by morning,
He wakens my ear to hear as the learned.
The Lord God has opened My ear,
and I was not rebellious, neither turned away back.
I gave My back to the smiters, and My cheeks to them that
plucked off the hair:
I hid not My face from shame and spitting.'

Isaiah 50:4-6 (KJV Modernized)

And finally we see this confirmed for us in the Gospel of Mark,

'Now in the morning, having risen a long while before daylight,
He went out and departed to a solitary place; and there He
prayed.'

Mark 1:35

Mystic Leaders

That the ancient path of true mysticism in the footsteps of Jesus was not limited to an apostolic first century, is confirmed by Paul's instruction to Timothy to select and appoint leaders (those that father others) from those who,

'...must possess the mystic secret of the faith [Christian truth as
hidden from ungodly men] with a clear conscience.'

1 Timothy 3:9 (AMP)

Instead of merely incorporating new converts into programs and church culture the Spirit of God wants us to give priority to experiencing the Divine presence through the mystical relationship opened by the blood of Jesus. Like those first disciples we are to be separated from the world once again as the people of '*THE WAY*' (1), and be marked by the miraculous (d). It is then, and only then that we will truly become the Elijah generation - fathers and sons - prepared to usher in the return of the Lord.

(d) Separation from the world: we are in the world but not of it. Elijah's '*the living God before whom I stand*' was his reality (1 Kings 17:1).

Separated from the world means we draw from heaven's reality not earth's facade.

(1) Acts 9:2.
(A) 2011, Taylor William C., *Practically Radical*, p. 32, Harper Collins Publishers, NY, USA.
(B) ZONDERVAN PUBLISHING HOUSE. *The Holy Bible*, The Berkeley Version in Modern English by Gerrit Verkuyl. The New Testament, Copyright © 1945 by Zondervan Publishing House.

Prayer:

Father, I want the world to know that You sent Jesus (John 17:21). Therefore, like Him, I desire to become one with You. Let my life also be a living expression of Your word to humanity. By Your grace empower me to enter Your presence by faith every day so that I too may bring a word in season to the weary. Amen.

Summary:

- Deja Vu is looking at something unfamiliar and feeling like you have experienced it before.

- These are spiritual excursions into our future.

- Vuja De is looking at the past to see how we got here.

- The resurgence of the Swiss watch industry has been based on past core values.

- The past can be an unrivalled source of revelation and strength for the future.

- 'Father's hearts to the children, children's hearts to their fathers' speaks of mature believers becoming humble and believers taking on the hearts of the apostolic fathers.

- Fathers are needed to release sons.

- Mysticism: the quest to experience the presence of God directly has the following tenets:
    - see the invisible God
    - become one with the infinite God
    - the word can become incarnate
    - layers within scripture
    - Hebrew letters, individually and in composition have meaning.

- John's gospel is mystic in nature.

- Leaders are to be drawn from those holding to a mystic faith.

Chapter 2

The Way of the Altar

Any discussion on the ancient paths must include looking at the Scriptural example of those who have made that journey. As Abraham is considered to be, 'the father of the faith', his life must provide keys to walking in union with God. In his lineage he is referred to as the man of the 'altar', his son Isaac is the man of the 'tent', his grandson, Jacob, is the man of the 'well', while his great grandson, Joseph, is the man of the 'kingdom'. The Apostle Paul makes reference to this godly line to assure us that all lovers of God are called with purpose,

> Who Am I?
>
> I met with God alone
> I had disciples
> I only said what God said
> I used parables
> I saw in the Spirit
> I said, 'God is not a man, that He should lie.'
>
> Answer: Page 15.

'...whom he did <u>predestinate</u>, them he also <u>called</u>: and whom he called, them he also <u>justified</u>: and whom he justified, them he also <u>glorified</u>.'

Romans 8:30 (KJV, Emphasis added)

(a) **Abraham's Altars:**

(Genesis 12:6-7): Abram, Shechem (Shoulder/Burden)

(Genesis 12:8): Bethel/ Ai (House of God/ Ruin)

(Genesis 13:3): Bethel (House of God)

(Genesis 13:18): He-bron (Union/Association)

(Genesis 15:10-18): Cut covenant

(Genesis 17:1): El Shaddai

(Genesis 17:5): Abra-ham (name change)

(Genesis 21:33): Beer Sheba, El Olam (Eter-nal God)

(Genesis 22:2): Mount Moriah, Jehovah Jireh (Lord sees/Lord pro-vides).

Though this progression assures us individually of the completeness of the plan of God in our lives, it is actually drawn from the lineage of Abraham. It was Abraham who was predestined, Isaac who was called, Jacob who was justified and Joseph who was glorified. Why is Abraham referred to as the man of the altar? Every time Abraham had an audience before God he made a sacrifice upon an altar and each altar site carries the name of the revelation that marked that encounter. The altars were stepping-stones in Abraham's progressive revelation of God (a). So important are the altars in Abraham's destiny that when he strays by going into Egypt he has to return to the altar between Bethel and Ai before he resumes his journey into the purposes of God (1). The altar is first a place of sacrifice, and subsequently, the place of fellowship with God. The shedding of innocent blood atones for sin and makes a way for audience before a Holy God.

Noah, who is described as a man 'who walked with God' (2), reveals that altars and sacrifice were, his path into the Presence of God (3). So important was sacrifice to Noah as the means for audience with God that he made future provision for acceptable sacrifice by taking into the ark not two but seven of every clean animal (4)!

According to the scriptural record Moses, the 'friend of God' (5), must also be considered a mystic who walked the ancient paths. He not only brought the Tablets of Stone to Israel after eighty days without food and water in God's presence on Mount Sinai (6) (b), but is also commended in the New Testament for, '*seeing Him who is invisible*' (7). Moses not only declares his utter daily dependence on God's presence (8), but also, like those before him, precedes his lone fellowship with God by sprinkling blood upon an altar (9)!

(b) Having separat-ed himself from the temporary pleasures of Egypt for a more enduring treasure (He-brews 11:24-26).

(1) Genesis 13:3. (2) Genesis 6:9. (3) Genesis 8:20. (4) Genesis 7:2. (5) Exodus 33:11. (6) Deuteronomy 9:11, 18, 25; 10:10. (7) Hebrews 11:27. (8) Exodus 33:15. (9) Exodus 24:4-8.

Even Balaam, provides evidence of the path to Eternity. If you can put his shortcomings aside for a moment, it is surprising to learn that he is described in Scripture as one who meets with God alone (1), has prophetic disciples (2), hears the voice of God (3), can only say what God says to him (4), speaks using God-inspired parables (5), and has the knowledge of The Most High (6)! It is also notable that when Jude mentions him in the New Testament he does so in the company of Cain and Korah, both of whom came from a godly line (7). It was Balaam, who brought forth timeless truth when he said,

> *'God is not a man, that he should lie;*
> *neither the son of man, that he should repent:*
> *hath he said, and shall he not make it good?'*

Numbers 23:19 (KJV)

So even though he is documented as succumbing to greed (8), the guy was no spiritual slouch either. He saw in the Spirit (9), experienced continuous open visions (10), and unlike many others (11), appears to take angelic encounters in his stride (12).

Some rightly point out that he was a soothsayer because of reference to divination in the text (13), and that he was duly killed because he showed Balak how to defile Israel (14). Hey there is no argument here! The point is, however, he was regularly in the Eternal realm. How did he get there? Like Noah, Abraham and Moses before him, Balaam found audience with God through sacrifice and the shedding of blood upon an altar (15).

The introduction of the tabernacle offerings in the wilderness under the direction of Moses was God's vehicle to re-establish the importance of sacrifice as 'the way' into His Presence (c).

(c) The Tabernacle corporately formalised sacrifice as a means of audience with God.

(1) Numbers 23:3, 15. (2) Numbers 22:22 cf. 2 Kings 3:11. (3) Numbers 24:16. (4) Numbers 22:38; 23:26; 24:13. (5) Numbers 23:5, 7ff; 23: 16, 18-24; 24:3-9. (6) Numbers 24:16. (7) Jude 11. (8) Jude 11. (9) Numbers 24:3, 15. (10) Numbers 24: 4, 16. (11) Judges 6:22-23; 13:21-22. (12) Numbers 22:33-34. (13) Numbers 23:23; 24:1. (14) Joshua 13:22; Revelation 2:14. (15) Numbers 23:1-3, 14, 29-30.

The ancient paths speak, both of the way through which we meet with a Holy God and also of those who have trodden that path in their desire for union with Him. It is evident that like the children of God in Jeremiah's time we are in need of renewing the ancient paths 'that make a way up' (1) into the heavenlies and need to diligently seek to *'find rest'* (2) in Him.

Why the emphasis on the altar? The altar as a place of sacrifice marks death and it is through death that we enter the eternal realm and are enlivened spiritually. Our lack of knowledge about ancient cultures means we readily miss the significance and role of sacrifice as a vehicle for audience with a deity. Of course, today Jesus is our personal sacrifice and His blood has made THE WAY for us into the one true God's presence. However, because of the many distractions present in our day we have all the more need to be 'diligent' to enter that place of rest by faith (3), coming boldly into the presence of God by the blood of Christ (4).

Entry Through Sacrifice

After Samson's parents met the angel of the LORD who declared they would have a child, the Bible records,

'So Manoah took a kid with a meat offering, and offered it upon a rock unto the Lord: and the angel did wondrously; and Manoah and his wife looked on.

For it came to pass, when the flame went up toward heaven from off the altar, that the angel of the Lord ascended in the flame of the altar. And Manoah and his wife looked on it, and fell on their faces to the ground.'

Judges 13:19-20 (KJV)

What we see here is that the angel stepped through their offering into the eternal realm. That offering is a prophetic picture of the death of Christ upon the cross. Similarly, when

(1) Jeremiah 18:15. (2) Jeremiah 6:16. (3) Hebrews 4:11; 10:20.
(4) Hebrews 4:16.

Jacob fled from his brother Esau he made camp overnight at Bethel and dreamed of a ladder set up on the earth that reached into heaven. Angels were ascending and descending upon it (1). It is provocative that they were not first descending and then ascending, but rather ascending and then descending (2). Why? You would think that angels would first come from the presence of God (descend) and then return there (ascend). In answer to our question Jesus Himself makes reference to this incident when speaking to Nathaniel,

> *'And He said to him, Truly, truly, I say to you, Hereafter you shall see heaven open, and the angels of God ascending and descending upon the Son of Man.'*

> John 1:51 (KJV Modernized)

In referencing Himself to Jacob's earlier dream, it would appear Jesus provides context on when heaven would be opened. While the word, 'hereafter' in English conveys the thought of, 'sometime after', it is better translated, 'from now'. In a sense, Jesus explained that He was operating under an open heaven. What needs to be remembered here is that Jesus prior to His death is harnessing the provision of His death by faith before it happens. Jacob's earlier encounter, which included seeing a ladder into heaven, was a prophetic forecast of what would happen through Jesus.

In Jacob's encounter with God he named the place, 'Bethel' which means, 'The House of God' and further recognized it as, 'The gate of heaven' (3). Jesus' use of the same incident declares that He is, 'The House of God' and the 'Eternal Gate' of heaven. Jacob turned upright the stone he had used as a pillow, making it into a pillar and then anointed it. That stone symbolized Christ. As 'sleep' in scripture is a parallel for 'death' (d), the stone in a horizontal position is a picture of Christ's death, and when it is moved to a vertical position it envisions His resurrection. Its

(d) Death as sleep. Hezekiah slept with his fathers (2 Chronicles 32:33)

David: lighten my eyes lest I sleep the sleep of death (Psalm 13:3)

Lazarus sleeping (John 11:3)

Paul: many weak and sickly among you and many sleep (1 Corinthians 11:29-30).

(1) Genesis 28:11-19. (2) Genesis 28:12. (3) Genesis 28:17.

(e) The scriptures tell us that Bethel had previously been called 'Luz' (Genesis 28:19). Luz means 'Almond', and the almond in scripture represents resurrection. For example, it was a dead or severed almond branch that budded and bore fruit to identify Aaron as High Priest (Numbers 17:8). The rod that budded is a type of Christ (Isaiah 11:1), once severed and then resurrected and now our High Priest interceding for us (Hebrews 4:14; 7:25, 26). Bethel is further shown as a place of death and resurrection in Abraham and Jacob both returning there after sojourns in the world (Genesis 13:3; 31:13; 35:1,3). Jacob also slept and awoke at Bethel which is also an action that can signify resurrection. To enter heaven via God's ancient paths the eternal traveller has to first pass through 'Bethel', that is he or she has personally to recognize the relevance of the blood of sacrifice shed at Calvary's cross for them.

subsequent anointing is God's approval of Christ as the Pillar and Cornerstone of the House of believers to be built around Him. This is after His sacrifice has made an ever-open path into the Presence of a Holy God (e).

Jacob's Ladder

The ladder is set up from earth to heaven, not from heaven to earth and angels ascend and then descend for a number of reasons. Firstly, the door had to be opened from our side through blood sacrifice (the way described above). As Adam, closed the door into the presence of God (1), Jesus, as the Son of Man, the last Adam (2) came to blast it off its hinges! Divine justice ensured that as was the judgment, so was the atonement (3). One man, barred us from God, the other opened a door that no man can shut (4). There is no other acceptable way for an audience with God. Jesus alone fulfilled all the criteria laid out in scripture for the Messiah, our earth-born Saviour (f), and true Kinsman-Redeemer (g). To consider any other path is to deny that God Himself lowered Himself to become a man, and as a sinless man, offered Himself to re-establish relationship with us (5).

Must be the Seed of the woman (Genesis 3:15)

Must be the Seed of the Abraham (Genesis 22:18)

Must be the tribe of Judah (Genesis 49:10)

Must be the House of David (Isaiah 9:07)

Must be born in Bethlehem (Micah 5:2)

Must be born of a virgin (Isaiah 7:14)

Must be God (Isaiah 9:6, Matthew 1:23)

(f) Requirements of the Messiah

When you read something in Scripture that doesn't make sense or, for that matter, if you see an anomaly in life (something out of place), it is a call to stop looking at it from this side and rather look at it from an eternal perspective.

We realize that the word, 'ascending' is not so much describing a physical 'rising', but rather a spiritual one.

(1) Genesis 3:24. (2) 1 Corinthians 15:45. (3) Romans 5:12-17; 1 Corinthians 15:21-22. (4) Revelation 3:7. (5) Philippians 2:6-8; 2 Corinthians 5:21; 1 John 4:9-10.

Angels ascending and descending is a description of entering and leaving the actual manifest Presence of God. The angel ascended in the flame before Manoah does so because worship is the door into His Presence. Angels ascend and descend on Christ because He is the eternal sacrifice made before the foundation of the world. He is the Ultimate act of worship being the Eternal Sacrifice and Door into the Father's Presence.

Going In and Out

When Jesus died for our sin, He truly became the Door of the sheep as recorded by John,

'I am the door: by me if any man enter in, he shall be saved, and shall go in and out, and find pasture.'

John 10:9 (KJV)

This verse explains that entry through the door of Christ is the passage to salvation. When we recognize that the sheepfold is a place of rest we see that this metaphor is a picture of entering the eternal realm of heaven. The mature Christian mystic enters 'in' to eternity by faith through the Blood of Christ and comes 'out' to minister. The word for 'pasture' used here means 'to feed'. This doesn't mean we go into heaven and then come into the world and feed on it. What it does mean is explained by the occasion where Jesus' disciples found Him ministering to the Samaritan woman. They asked Him to eat and He replied,

'... I have meat to eat that you know not of. Therefore said the disciples one to another, Has any man brought him anything to eat? Jesus said to them, My meat is to do the will of him that sent me, and to finish his work.'

John 4:32-34 (KJV Modernized)

Our food, like that of Christ, is to do the Father's will, which

(g) kinsman-redeemer definition: goel (Ruth 3:13)

(H1350) The word means to act as a redeemer for a deceased family member; to buy back a kinsman's possessions (Leviticus 25:26); to redeem or buy back from bondage (Leviticus 25:48); to avenge a kinsman's murder (Numbers 35:19); to redeem an object through a payment (Leviticus 27:13). This word is used to convey God's redemption of individuals from spiritual death and His redemption of the nation of Israel from Egyptian bondage (see Exodus 6:6).

is disclosed in His presence (h).

(h) Mystical union is not just self indulgent separation but also has an outworking of what is received in the secret place. It is a going 'in' AND coming 'out'.

The scriptures confirm that those, who are wrongly motivated are capable of entering the spiritual realms,

'Truly, truly, I say unto you, He that enters not by the door into the sheepfold, but climbs up some other way, the same is a thief and a robber.'

John 10:1 (KJV Modernized)

Those who enter any other way, for their own gain, or selfish ambition, are effectively pawns of satan (1). Like satan before them they are marked with self effort and spiritual pride as depicted in their 'climbing up' (2). This verse also speaks loudly in what it doesn't say! It says that 'love', the opposite of selfish gain, and 'humility', the opposite of pride, are essential travel companions for those making the journey.

Where do the Ancient Paths take us?

The ancient paths lead us from the confines of this world. Our world can be thought of as existing in three dimensions, everything has length, width and depth. However, the Apostle Paul added the word 'height' to the equation. He prayed that the Ephesians would know the love of Christ that could go beyond earthly constraints,

'May be able to comprehend with all the saints what is the <u>*width*</u> *and* <u>*length*</u> *and* <u>*depth*</u> *and* <u>*height*</u> *to know the love of Christ which passes knowledge....'*

Ephesians 3:18-19 (Emphasis added)

In entering the eternal 'heights' we are able to partake of things beyond worldly comprehension, things that are outside our normal intellectual knowledge. This higher and eternal kingdom that has been opened to us is centered in Him, who is love. It manifests in acts done for others in the

(1) John 8:44a; 10:10. (2) Isaiah 14:12-15.

greatest extravagance of love, for love is other-centeredness. The ultimate expression of love is displayed in God dying in our place for the sins of humanity. Jesus' 'love as strong as death' is the unseen truth behind all of the multiplication miracles in scripture (1).

Provision

The widow of Zarephath gave up her last meal to Elijah to be sustained throughout the drought with a barrel of meal and a cruse of oil that did not run dry (2). She also happens to be a preview of the consecrated church receiving faith's reward through the cross. Similarly, when Elisha reached into heaven to provide a river of oil from one pot he drew from an eternal well yet to be opened in Christ (3). Finally, Jesus in turning water into wine (4), bringing forth a miracle draught of fish (5) and multiplying the loaves and fishes (6) is also tapping into a warehouse of provision that was yet to be opened in the cross.

Inter-dimensionality

Mystic journeys are hinted at in Obadiah's request for assurance that Elijah will not translocate before he has a chance to bring King Ahab to him (7), by Elijah's outrunning Ahab's chariot (8), and ultimately, like Enoch before him, by Elijah's transmigration permanently to heaven (9).

In the New Testament it is witnessed in Philip being caught away by the Spirit from the Ethiopian eunuch only to be found in Azotus preaching the gospel (10). And according to my good friend Adam F. Thompson it is this timelessness, that places Moses with Christ on the Mount of Transfiguration, only to descend from Mount Sinai unaware that his face carries the glory of it some 1400 years earlier (11)!

Recent reports of people entering into elevators and appearing in other countries when they stepped out, of

(1) Song of Songs 8:6. (2) 1 Kings 17:11-16. (3) 2 Kings 4:1-7. (4) John 2:9. (5) John 21:6, 11. (6) John 6:5-14. (7) 1 Kings 18:11-12. (8) 1 Kings 18:46. (9) Genesis 5:24; 2 Kings 2:11-12. (10) Acts 8:39-40. (11) Exodus 34:29.

speakers appearing in two places at the same time and of others travelling immense distances in what was a blink of an eye are on the increase. A new generation of mystics dissatisfied with earthly limitations, are emerging to usher in a new type of 'normal'. The ancient paths are being rediscovered.

The point of all of this is that we have been granted the privilege of entering heaven into the presence of Almighty God. Jesus died to open that door of opportunity. God's table of provision lies beckoning us in. We cannot afford to be like the lazy man, who having put forth his hand to take hold of provision fails to lift it to his mouth (1). To fail to enter in would be tantamount to the greatest travesty ever (2)!

(1) Proverbs 19:24. (2) Hebrews 2:3.

Prayer:

Father, I now realize the relevance of sacrifice as the path into Your presence. I recognize the many distractions that keep me out of the secret place. However, I will be diligent to enter boldly through the curtain opened by faith through the precious Blood of Your dear Son; that having entered 'in' I may also go 'out' to do Your will. Amen.

Summary:

- Abraham's altars are stepping-stones in his spiritual journey.

- The altar is a place of sacrifice and then fellowship with God.

- Abraham, Noah, Moses and Balaam were all mystics who found audience with God through sacrifice.

- The ancient paths speak both of the way into the presence of God and those who have trodden it.

- There is a need for a renewing of the ancient paths, that 'make a way up' and 'find rest' in Him.

- Death is the way into eternity.

- Jesus' death is our opportunity to enter into God's presence.

- Angels, similarly, have access through Jesus' act of worship in laying down His life.

- Mystics enter 'in' by faith through the Blood of Christ and come 'out' to minister.

- Our world exists in three dimensions, through Christ's love a fourth is opened to us.

- Mystic inter-dimensional excursions are on the increase as the ancient paths are rediscovered.

- Not entering in to what has been opened through Christ's sacrifice borders on criminal neglect.

Chapter 3

Portals of Heaven

Many people question the validity and purpose of the manifestations of gold teeth, gold dust, gemstones and manna appearing in Christian meetings (a). There are scriptural grounds to understand these events as simply God's glorious kingdom manifesting through people acting as conduits between heaven and earth. It is setting the stage for outpourings of heaven the like of which have never been seen before.

'The kingdom of God does not come with observation; Nor will they say, "See here!" or "See there!" For indeed, the kingdom of God is within you.'

Luke 17:20-21

When Jesus spoke these words he was not referring to harnessing our personal inner resources, to see things through.

(a) This is a phenomenon happening worldwide.

See *The Finger of God* DVD

Wanderlust productions, a Darren Wilson film, www.fingerofgodfilm.com

Neither was He suggesting that we tap into an innate goodness or some nebulous universal power within by promoting thoughts of 'peace' and 'love' toward our fellow man. What He reveals here is that our hearts are the portals through which the kingdom of God is manifest!

The True Temple

When Moses made the Tabernacle in the wilderness he did so under strict instruction from God, to follow the pattern which was shown him on the mountain (1). The Book of Hebrews equates the mountain with heaven (2). Thus the earthly Tabernacle, which became the Temple - when Israel moved into occupying the Promised Land - was modelled on the throne of God in heaven. To come before the mercy seat here on earth in the Temple was to come before God in heaven. There was, as it were, a 'portal' in the Spirit between the two places.

John's Gospel takes us further in God's plan for the portal He had established by indirectly revealing Jesus' mission on earth. It is early in his Gospel that John captures Jesus cleansing the Temple (3). This is in stark contrast to the synoptic Gospels (Matthew, Mark, Luke), where Jesus is shown to be cleansing the Temple at the close of His earthly ministry (4). The two incidents become bookends of what is known in Hebrew poetic form as 'inclusio', 'inclusion' or 'enveloping'. This literary device is used throughout scripture to bring 'focus to' or 'contain' a theme or subject. For example, Psalm Eight starts and finishes with the same verse, and the Beatitudes open and close with, '...*for theirs is the kingdom of heaven*' (5) to bring focus to their subject matter. Jesus, by beginning and closing His ministry with the cleansing of the Temple, was declaring His mission: He came to cleanse the true earthly temples (b). It is

(b) Jesus' mission was to reunite God and Man which required dealing with the sin issue and cleansing the human temple.

(1) Exodus 25:40. (2) Hebrews 8:5. (3) John 2:14-18. (4) Matthew 21:12-13; Mark 11:15-17; Luke 19:45-46. (5) Matthew 5:3, 10.

John again, who dares to take us deeper by documenting Jesus' proclamation,

'Destroy this temple, and in three days I will raise it up.'

John 2:19

In doing so, John provides us with the opportunity to see that Jesus was not merely talking of the Temple made of stone, but rather His own body (1), which was the prototype of the temple and 'earthen' altar within all believers. John not only provides the missing piece for us to understand Jesus' purpose in the early cleansing of the temple, he also is the first within the Canon of Scripture to explain the thought that the human spirit is the 'holy ground' on which God and man meet. Our bodies are now truly the temple of God and our spirit is the 'secret place' or the 'place of meeting' with the invisible God, and as such it is the portal through which heaven finds expression on earth!

Dual Citizenship

Jesus' discussion with Nicodemus unfolds for us an important insight into the nature of a spirit in right relationship with God. John records Nicodemus's difficulty in comprehending the spiritual truths Jesus unfolds (2). Finally, He says,

'If I told you earthly things and you do not believe, how will you believe if I tell you heavenly things? No one has ascended to heaven but He <u>who came down from heaven</u>, that is, the Son of Man <u>who is in heaven.</u>'

John 3:12-13 (Emphasis added)

Earlier in the conversation Nicodemus had acknowledged that no one could do what Jesus was doing without being in harmony with God (3). Now, in this verse, he learns that in being one with God, Jesus was in heaven and on earth at the same

---

(1) John 2:21. (2) John 3:10. (3) John 3:2.

time. Wow! And the same is true of us. How do we know? Well, the New Testament informs us that those who are joined to the Lord are one Spirit (1), and then, in Jesus' 'High Priestly' prayer with His Father we read His request that our oneness would parallel His own with the Father,

> '*Holy Father, keep through Your name those whom You have given Me, That <u>they may be one as We are</u>.*'

John 17:11 (Emphasis added)

As Jesus was one with the Father and thereby coexisted on earth and in heaven at the same time, we now similarly exist in both realms by faith. Extraordinary? Yes, but nonetheless true. We have dual citizenship with heaven as our primary residence (2). This of course is confirmed in Paul's letter to the Ephesian church that pronounces we are now seated in heavenly places in Him (3). Jesus' conversation with Nicodemus provides us with a 'Vuja de' moment in the lives of Enoch and Elijah. In telling us that, '*no one has ascended to heaven but He who came down from heaven*' (4), He indirectly reveals that Enoch and Elijah, as those the Bible records as having entered heaven while living, must have had a revelation of the cross before its time. That's right, in order for them to 'qualify' according to this verse, they must have been 'in Him'. This means that our spiritual fathers walked the same ancient path, as we do, purely by faith in the finished work of Christ upon the cross, before it had happened. The Book of Hebrews speaking about Enoch adds,

> '<u>*By faith*</u> *Enoch was taken away so that he did not see death, "and was not found, because God had taken him"; for before he was taken he had this testimony, that he pleased God.*
>
> *But without faith it is impossible to please Him, for he who <u>comes to God must believe that He is</u>, and that He is a rewarder of those who diligently seek Him.*'

Hebrews 11:5-6 (Emphasis added)

(1) 1 Corinthians 6:17. (2) John 17:16. (3) Ephesians 2:6. (4) John 3:13.

This verse further explains that Enoch was a person who continuously sought to be in the presence of the invisible God. It was his practice of shutting out the world to meet with God in the sanctuary of his own heart and godly imagination which pleased God. Or as the text simply has it, *'By faith...comes to God, believing that He is'*.

Seeing Precedes Speaking

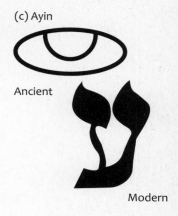

(c) Ayin

Ancient

Modern

The sixteenth letter of the Hebrew alphabet is the letter Ayin (c). Its name means 'eye' and as such it stands for sight, perception and insight. Technically, in Hebrew 'Ayin' means an aperture, a source and a spring of water. By way of example, when Israel came out of Egypt they came to Elim *'where there were twelve springs (Ayin) of water'* (1). Just as it makes sense in the natural that an eye becomes a spring of water when an emotional chord is struck, so there is a deeper truth housed in this simple Hebrew letter that is even more relevant spiritually. What we 'see' on the canvas of our spirit - the core of our being - is to be the basis for the water of words (2) that subsequently come out of our mouths. That is 'seeing' precedes 'speaking'.

This is an important spiritual mystery. A mystery to which the church appears to be slowly awakening. The sign that a new day has come is seen in the Body of Christ shaking off the bedclothes of indifference it has shown toward dreams and visions. We are now realizing that dreams and visions are not just fuel for the prophetic clique within the church (d). They are major channels for God to communicate what is happening in the Spirit to EVERY Christian. Jesus died that we may receive His Spirit, His Spirit is marked by prophecy - the ability to speak what God wants to say in a given situation - and the major vehicle for prophecy, you guessed it, is dreams and visions (3). As we have seen in the Hebrew letter 'Ayin', seeing proceeds speaking. Further to this, Jesus told Nicodemus that 'seeing'

(d) See the book:

The Divinity Code to understanding your dreams and visions

Isbn:
978-0-7684-4090-4

Ebook:
978-0-7684-8878-4

(1) Exodus 15:27. (2) Ephesians 5:26. (3) Acts 2:17-18.

was a necessary prelude to 'entering' the kingdom (1). Speaking brings what we are seeing to the door of our lips, and through them, heaven finds entry into the earthly realm. That means that if we are not 'seeing', we are not yet empowered to be speaking, and if we are not speaking then we most certainly are not truly 'entering' into what God has for us!

A 'word' received visually to our spirit carries tremendous spiritual authority and as such, does not, *'fall to the ground'* (2). These are 'words' that, *'proceed from the mouth of the LORD'* not only to feed Israel in the wilderness but to instil in them that they cannot live without them (3). This is what Jesus described as *'spirit'* and *'life'* (4), they are the 'rhema' sword of the Spirit (5), and the true *'words of our testimony'*, given that we may overcome (6) (e).

(e) For the difference between rhema and logos see chapter 6, page 71.

One time I was teaching on dream interpretation in Canberra, Australia's capital city. A woman named, Maggie, asked to recount her young daughter's dream for interpretation. In the dream the young girl and her sister were in their room when the walls fell down and they found themselves standing on a pile of rocks. Out from under the pile of rocks slithered a big multi-colored python-type snake. The snake frightened the girls, so they ran away from it to stand by a river. As they were running lots of little snakes came out of the big snake. At that moment, the girl who had the dream said she realized that it was no longer her sister standing next to her, but her little brother Benjamin. Benjamin wasn't afraid of the snake. He walked up to it, looked it in the eyes and it exploded and was destroyed. Based on the dream and the insight it revealed I declared that Maggie and her household were about to be delivered from a generational spirit. She had started walking forward down the aisle, when she suddenly fell to the floor writhing like a snake. She was delivered there and then.

(1) John 3:3-5. (2) 1 Samuel 3:19. (3) Deuteronomy 8:3. (4) John 6:63.
(5) Ephesians 6:17. (6) Revelation 12:11.

Benjamin, which means, 'Son of my right hand' was not merely the younger brother, but a metaphor for her 'brother' Jesus (1), who on seeing the snake took authority over it and cast it out. On the basis of God's word, which came in the form of a dream and its interpretation, authority was granted to me, to set her and her family free.

The story didn't finish there because the next day I was invited to a barbecue, which Maggie and her girls attended. As I was standing talking to a group of people, Maggie came up to me with her hands outstretched and said, 'For the man of God' and presented me with a plate of food. Quite honestly I felt like turning around to see to whom she was talking. Ten minutes later she returned with a drink, saying the same thing, and then again a bit later with a chair for me to sit upon. This time she said, 'Last night, pastor, I had a dream. And in that dream my family and I were in a prison, it was dark, and people were doing all sorts of sordid things, some were using drugs, others having sex, etc. My family and I tried to get out of this dark place, but the guards were harsh and kept us in this place. Suddenly the Holy Spirit came and picked us up and lifted us over the walls of the prison and set us down on the other side. A different guard dressed in gold came forward and said, "Now you can go free!"' The dream Maggie shared at the barbecue was what had taken place the day before.

In ourselves we are nothing, but in Him, we are the very 'Stargate' for Him to manifest Himself here on earth. All Glory to God!

That 'seeing' proceeds 'speaking' is a point that John echoes repeatedly in relating insights into the life of Christ,

'We <u>speak</u> what We know and testify what We have <u>seen</u>.'

John 3:11 (Emphasis added)

(1) Hebrews 2:11.

31

'And what He has <u>seen</u> and heard, that He <u>testifies</u>....'

John 3:32 (Emphasis added)

'For the Father loves the Son, and <u>shows</u> Him all things that He Himself does.'

John 5:20 (Emphasis added)

'I <u>speak</u> what I have <u>seen</u> with My Father....'

John 8:38 (Emphasis added)

'The words that I <u>speak</u> to you, I do not <u>speak</u> on My own....'

John 14:10 (Emphasis added)

And finally,

'The <u>word</u> which you hear is not Mine but the Father's Who sent Me.'

John 14:24 (Emphasis added)

As outlined in the previous chapter Jesus earnestly spent time with the Father, and his active, anticipatory hunger drew a response of spiritually inspired insights that empowered Him to manifest the kingdom in all that He spoke and did. Oh, how the world is awaiting other mature sons to arise (1)!

Joshua's Carbon Footprint

The Old Testament provides us with the perfect example of how this is outworked. When Joshua was about to enter the Promised Land, God said to him,

'Every place that the <u>sole</u> of your foot will tread upon I have given you....'

Joshua 1:3 (Emphasis added)

(1) Romans 8:19.

The word here for 'sole' is the Hebrew word, 'Kaph' it describes 'a cupped hand' and that is how this letter was drawn in its original Hebrew form (f). The word is used to describe a cupped hand, a spoon, palm fronds, and also the sole of the foot. It principally describes a hollow or a concave form. At this point you need to appreciate that the human heart is described within scripture as a hollow or concave form, that is why David writes, *'My cup overflows'* (1), believers are *'filled'* (2), and why, *'Deep calls to deep'* (3). So when God says, *'every place that the sole of your foot will tread'* He is not talking about the mere physical act of claiming new territory, He is describing a deeper spiritual truth that parallels that act. It is that every revelation placed in our heart by God is the foundation of our next step into claiming our Promised Land! We move into the destiny that God has for us a step at a time, putting the weight of our belief on these daily deposits of revelation.

Heaven is the World to Come

My wife and I attended a wedding ceremony recently which appeared to be quite normal in proceedings, basically walking through the vows with some Bible teaching about love and marriage to help anchor the civil ceremony. I thought the service was running to schedule until the minister concluded his teaching by saying something like, '...and if both of you live good lives before God you will go to heaven when you die'. Those words shook me out of my social passivity to realize that this leader, did not understand that we possess eternal life now (g)! Certainly, there are scriptures which could be interpreted that we do await heaven in its fullness, for example,

'Truly, I say to you, there is no one who has left house, or parents, or brothers, or wife, or children, for the sake of the kingdom of God. Who will not receive many times more in

(f) Kaph

Ancient

Modern

Kaph:
(H3709) kap: A feminine noun meaning hand, the flat of the hand, the flat of the foot, hollow, bent. The principal meaning is hollow, often used of the hollow of the physical hand or foot. It also relates to cupped or bent objects such as spoons (Numbers 7:80). In metaphysical overtones, Job declared his cleanness of hand (Job 9:30); and David linked clean hands with a pure heart (Psalm 24:4).

(g) And taught that we earn it by good living!

(1) Psalm 23:5. (2) Acts 2:4. (3) Psalm 42:7.

this present time, and <u>in the world to come</u> everlasting life.'

Luke 18:29-30 (KJV Modernized, Emphasis added)

On the surface, it appears that this scripture points to futuristically stepping into eternity, and yet, elsewhere in scripture it is suggested that believers have eternal life now,

'For God so loved the world, that He gave His only begotten Son, that whosoever believes in Him should not perish, but <u>have</u> everlasting life.'

John 3:16 (Emphasis added)

And again,

'Truly, truly I say unto you, He that hears My word, and believes on Him that sent Me, <u>has</u> everlasting life, and shall not come into condemnation; but is passed from death unto life.'

John 5:24 (KJV Modernized, Emphasis added)

In this last example the word 'has', not 'will have' is used to indicate that the process is in the present i.e. NOW! Other scriptures confirm this present reality,

'Therefore if any man be in Christ, he is a new creature: old things are passed away; behold, all things are become new.'

2 Corinthians 5:17 (KJV)

The moment we accept Christ and His vicarious sacrifice for our sins we are 'born again' of the Spirit of God and enter into eternal life. Therefore, how do we reconcile these two apparently contrasting aspects of eternal life? Is it now or in the future? The answer to both these questions is, 'Yes!' The two are actually compatible and not mutually exclusive. In the same way as we are now seated in heavenly places (1), and yet

(1) Ephesians 2:6.

on earth in these earthly tents both at the same time. So we have entered the eternal realm now and there is also a future consummation that awaits us. Think about it, if it were solely a futuristic fulfilment that we looked forward to, then 'death' would be our saviour.

That the 'present' and 'the world to come' are not mutually exclusive can be seen in scriptures that show we can partake of the future today. The writer to the Hebrews warned infant believers that by experiencing displays of the power of the Holy Spirit they had partaken of *'the world to come'* and should be careful not to turn aside from the journey they had begun,

> *'For it is impossible for those who were once enlightened, and have tasted of the heavenly gift, and were made partakers of the Holy Ghost, And* <u>*have tasted the good word*</u> *of God, and* <u>*the powers of the world to come.*</u> *If they should fall away....'*

> Hebrews 6:4-6 (KJV, Emphasis added)

The 'good word' spoken of here in the Greek text that the new believers had 'tasted' is the 'rhema' word. In partaking of this 'living bread' from heaven they had sampled the promises of God that heaven had laid up. In other words, they had stepped outside of time in entering heaven's storehouse as 'eagles' eating from Christ's body (1) and brought 'tomorrow's' provision into 'today'! Every time we enter heaven - the eternal realm - we enter the world to come (h).

This is how Moses can climb Mount Sinai in the wilderness to be in God's presence and step into an encounter with Christ and His disciples on the Mount of Transfiguration which took place 1400 years later. This is why, at the wedding in Cana, Jesus replied to His mother *'Woman, what have I to do with you? My hour has not yet come'* (2), but He still went ahead and turned the water into wine. Of course, the reference to His *'hour not*

(h) Heaven: the world to come. Why should we be surprised to learn that heaven is *'the world to come'*? Didn't heaven fore-tell Christ's birth for the Magi (Matthew 2:2)? Didn't Jesus say the sky foretold to-morrow's weather (Matthew 16:2-3)? And didn't Joel say that the Heavens would again warn us of Christ's return (Joel 2:31)?

(1) Luke 17:37. (2) John 2:4.

(i) The Talmud (the Jewish commentary on the Torah), teaches that the Sabbath is a semblance of the world to come (Berachos 57b). We need to recognize here that the Sabbath is not a day, it is a person! The Person of the Lord Jesus Christ, as He is our Rest (Matthew 11:28; Ephesians 2:14; Hebrews 4:1,3), He is the Day of salvation (Exodus 14:13; Psalm 25:5; 68:19; 71:15; Isaiah 49:8; Luke 19:9; 2 Corinthians 6:2), and He is our Jubilee (Leviticus 25:10, 13, Isaiah 61:1-2).

(j) Being conduits for a God *who calls things which do not exist as though they did* (Romans 4:17).

yet come' was a reference to His death (1). Therefore, the miracle that He performed was a prophetic enactment of His being offered to God, and believers subsequently being filled with the wine of the Holy Spirit. It should be evident then that on that day the wedding guests who 'tasted' the wine were experiencing something of the world to come. And again, when Jesus delivered the Syrophenician woman's daughter it was not yet time for Gentiles to partake of the benefits of Christ's ministry, however her persistence, pierced through eternity and took what was reserved for the future (2). Another example is when Jesus forgave the woman caught in adultery. He did so on the basis of what He was about to achieve at Calvary (3) (i).

Just as Jacob saw angels ascending and descending upon a ladder at a place he called Bethel, which means, 'The House of God' (4), we need to realize that as the house or temple of God, we also are portals into the eternal realm. Our spiritual man is the upper end of the ladder and our mouths the vehicles for God (j) as its point of contact with earth.

Suddenly, what we know as 'the Lord's prayer' has new meaning, when we pray,

'Your kingdom come. Your will be done on earth as it is in heaven.'

Matthew 6:10

It is not so very surprisingly that the Lord's instruction on prayer is preceded with the need to leave earth behind by shutting the door and entering into the 'unseen realm' or 'secret place' of heaven (5). There, according to the above verse, we become portals or conduits of what is already existing in heaven. Everyone of us has a role in ushering heaven to earth. Everyone can see *'the world to come'* materialize.

(1) cf John 5:25, 28; 7:30; 8:29: 12:23; 27; 13:1; 17:1. (2) Mark 7:26-30 cf. Matthew 11:12. (3) John 8:3-11. (4) Genesis 28:10-17. (5) Matthew 6:6.

Gold teeth, gold dust, gemstones and manna are not phenomenon to derail us. They are weird, but only through earthbound eyes. As portals of heaven God is preparing us for so much more. Rather than questioning the validity of weird happenings it would be better to ask what is God communicating through their manifestation? They are simply basic-level kingdom outpourings. Their appearance witness to heaven's inter-dimensional provision so that faith may arise in God's people for 'greater works'.

Prayer:

Father, I understand that Your kingdom is manifest on earth through human beings. Like Enoch, I seek Your face. Allow me to 'see' what you are doing, so that I may 'speak' accordingly. Amen.

Summary:

- Our hearts are the portals through which the kingdom of God is manifest.
- Jesus' mission was to reunite God and Man which required dealing with the sin issue and cleansing the human temple.
- Jesus was in heaven and on earth at the same time.
- We have the same dual citizenship.
- Seeing precedes speaking.
- Every revelation placed in your heart by God is the foundation for the next step in claiming your Promised Land.
- We move into the promises of God a revelatory step at a time.
- Heaven is the world to come.
- Every believer has a role in ushering heaven to earth to see '*the world to come*' manifest.

The Mystic Awakening

Subject Landscape & Chapter Milestones

YOU ARE HERE

Man. Utd. 4

Heaven is the World to come •
Move into Kingdom one revelation step at a time •
Seeing precedes speaking •
(John 3:13) Dual Citizenship •
Man: The True Temple •
(Luke 17:21) The Kingdom Within •

Portals of Heaven

3 P. 25

Inter-dimensionality •
Super-abundant provision •
Need to go 'in' and 'out' •
Jesus is Jacob's ladder •
Entry Through Sacrifice •
Tabernacle •
Balaam •
Moses •
Noah •
Abraham •

2 P. 13

The Way of the Altar

Mystics •
-David
-John
-Jesus
Mystic Tenets •
- See Invisible God
- One with God
- Word Incarnate
- Layers in Scripture
- Letters convey message
Ancient Paths
(Malachi 4:6) Spirit of Elijah
- Fathers -> Sons
- Sons -> Fathers
Wrong Trends •
Vu Ja de •
De Ja Vu •

1 P. 1

Back to the Future

What Balaam Saw
Numbers 24:2

North
Leviticus 1:11
Psalm 48:2
Isaiah 14:13

East
Genesis 2:8
Numbers 2:3
Ezra 47:2
10:19
43:1-4
Zechariah 14:4
Matthew 2:1-2
24:27

N North

W   E

S

Numbers 2:9 (E)
(Lion) Judah 186, 400

Numbers 2:16 (S)
(Man) Reuben 151,450

Numbers 2 :24 (W)
(Ox) Ephraim 108,100

Numbers 2:31 (N)
(Eagle) Dan 157,600

Introduction •

Chapter 4

Man. Utd.

Recently, a friend I have been corresponding with for a couple of years sent me a request to help him interpret a dream that he had. While most would not pay too much attention to such a simple, obviously topical and apparently insignificant dream there is in it a deep revelation that God would have for all of us. The email read,

'Can you help me with this dream? I saw a football match between Manchester United and Sunderland which ended in a 1-1 draw, Sunderland scored through Asamoah Gyan in the 2nd minute while Man. Utd. equalised through Sun Park in the 53rd minute.'

Much of what God communicates through dreams and visions is metaphoric. They come as personal parables using topics in which the individual has some interest. This is one of the reasons why we often miss their significance; the natural man associates the content with recent activity - a movie we saw, a sport we played or something that captured our attention during the day - and is prone to discount them as simply the brain doing its daily 'tidy up'.

To understand the dream and its importance we first need to explore a dynamic that is foundational to us as spirit beings. Most born-again believers would be familiar with the following verse,

'That if you confess with thy <u>mouth</u> the Lord Jesus, and believe in your <u>heart</u> that God has raised Him from the dead, you shall be saved. For with the <u>heart</u> man believes unto righteousness; and with the <u>mouth</u> confession is made unto salvation.'

Romans 10:9-10 (KJV Modernized, Emphasis added)

This verse is used and understood by most evangelical Christians as an essential component of spiritual conversion. And rightly so. The word, *'salvation'* used here is the Greek word, 'Sozo'. It is used 54 times in the New Testament. In only twenty of these it relates to what we call, 'spiritual salvation' (a). In twenty of the remaining thirty-four occasions it relates to the rescue of physical life from some impending peril or instant death (b), while in the other fourteen the inference is to deliverance from disease or demon possession (c).

Isn't it interesting that we see the need for the heart and the mouth to be in alignment for spiritual salvation, and yet, fail to recognize its importance in the areas of sickness, disease and deliverance? We have also made a distinction between what we call 'eternal salvation' and these other two areas where the word, 'Sozo' is used. Healing and deliverance are

Scriptures where sozo (G4982) used:

(a) twenty times the reference is to spiritual salvation: (Matthew 1:21; 10:22; 19:25; 24:13, 22; Mark 8:35; 10:26; 13:13, 20; 16:16; Luke 7:50; 8:12; 9:24; 13:23; 18:26; 19:10; John 3:17; 5:34; 10:9; 12:47).

(b) In twenty instances the inference is to the rescue of physical life: (Matthew 8:25; 14:30; 16:25; 27:40, 42, 49; Mark 8:35; 15:30, 31; Luke 9:24, 56; 23:35, 37, 39; John 12:27).

(c) Fourteen times 'sozo' relate to deliverance from disease or demon possession: (Matthew 9:21, 22; Mark 3:4; 5:23, 28, 34; 6:56; 10:52; Luke 6:9; 8:36, 48, 50; 17:19; 18:42; John 11:12).

also equal manifestations of entering heaven. Jesus pointed out that there was no such distinction, when He said,

'Why do you reason these things in your hearts? Which is easier, to say to the paralytic, "Your sins are forgiven you," or to say, "Arise, take up your bed and walk"?'

Mark 2:8-9

Truth

The word used for 'truth' in the New Testament is the Greek word, 'Aletheia'. It means 'the unveiled reality lying at the basis of, and agreeing with, an appearance'. Like two tumblers on a lock, 'truth' is when both tumblers line up and the lock pops open. In relation to the word, 'Sozo' we could say that if the heart and the mouth are not in alignment, then what is coming out of the mouth is not truth. How important is this? James captures its gravity when he says,

Truth: Aletheia

(G0225), *'the unveiled reality lying at the basis of, and agreeing with, an appearance'*

'Let him ask in faith, nothing wavering. For he that wavers is like a wave of the sea driven with the wind and tossed. For let not that man think that he shall receive any thing of the Lord. A double minded man is unstable in all his ways.'

James 1:6-8 (KJV Modernized)

A double-minded man is one whose mouth and heart do not line up. According to these verses the product of such division is fruitlessness. The tragic Old Testament example is a nation stuck in no-man's-land, unable to move into the Promised Land because Egypt is still their reference point.

How do we get the head and the heart to line up? The prescribed remedy is to encourage the Christian to

Who Am I?

*I was a double-minded man
I eventually defeated the enemy as 'one man'
By getting my mouth in line with my heart
Revealing the glory of God*

Answer: Page 46 ff.

43

meditate on the written word of God, so that as he ponders on the Scriptures on a particular subject he will receive revelation to his heart. This is based on such scriptures as,

> *'Blessed is the man... his delight is in the law of the LORD, and in His law he meditates day and night.*
> *He shall be like a tree... and whatever he does shall prosper.'*
>
> Psalm 1:1-3

And,

> *'This Book of the Law shall not depart from your mouth, But you shall meditate in it day and night, That you may observe to do according to all that is written in it. For then you will make your way prosperous and then you will have good success.'*
>
> Joshua 1:8

(d) Visualization is as real to our soul as an earthly event. Simulation by vizualization is used extensively by athletes, pilots and therapists to visit an experience and reduce anxiety and assist cognitive response. Visiting a situation beforehand via simulation provides a framework or model into which we are able to step.

This method works. What we meditate on has greater influence over us than life itself (d). Therefore, if we visualize kingdom realities as portrayed through scripture we will transcend our earthly limitations (e)!

(e) Psalm 1 speaks of not walking, standing or sitting with ungodly, sinners and scoffers respectively as a prelude to entering the blessings of God. Each stance (walking, standing...) and personality (ungodly, sinner...) combine to outline the path to spiritual degeneration.

Meditation on the written word provides the framework of the kingdom we are called to enter by faith. Using the imagination, the panorama provided by Old Testament passages begin to open and produce fruit; when New Testament keys of understanding are applied (f). Invariably, the key that opens these passages is Christ, and in particular, the cross.

(f) The Gospels are technically OT up until the death of Christ.

However, for those who take a purely intellectual approach, meditation can equate to the head trying to change the heart, when in fact, it is God who gives revelation and gives it to the heart (1). For example, a person can memorize a Book of the Bible and yet not know God. For others, meditation is prone

(1) Matthew 16:16-17; John 1:12-13.

44

to the corruption of idolatry (1), in making the word to say what its readers want it to say. What needs to be appreciated, particularly in the first of the two passages quoted above, is that the word, *'law'* is broader than just the written word of God. It is rather captivating to find that the most common use for the root of the word deals with shooting arrows, sending rain AND giving instruction. So while the primary use of the actual Hebrew word, 'Torah', translated *'law'*, is teaching (g), yet, on a more fundamental level, meditation is contemplation and muttering the 'word' which comes from His presence, like the rain out of heaven, or as an arrow to the heart.

(g) The passage from the Psalms is understood to be that of meditating in His instruction, which incorporates the written code called *'the Law'*.

The second passage from Joshua definitely deals with meditation in the writings of Moses and in particular, the Book of Deuteronomy. Here the process of meditation on the written Law was designed so that the people would make the given directives an integral part of their lifestyle. In this manner Israel was to be kept and set apart unto God so that the Messiah could come. However, Jeremiah says there was coming a day when God would establish a new covenant with Israel in which the law would be written on the heart,

> *'But this is the covenant that I will make with the house of Israel after those days, says the LORD: I will put My law in their minds, and write it on their hearts; and I will be their God, and they shall be My people.'*

> Jeremiah 31:33

This event would be so transformational that, according to the next verse, every person would be given opportunity to know God,

> *'No more shall every man teach his neighbour, and every man his brother, saying, 'Know the LORD,' for they all shall know*

(1) Ezekiel 14:4.

> *Me, from the least of them to the greatest of them....'*
>
> Jeremiah 31:34

Think about that: the new relationship was going to remove social, economic, educational and ecclesiastical status, which meant it was not going to come through outward observance and intellectual pursuit. That's right! In instituting the new covenant, God was going to impart understanding of His will to the inner man and it would flow outward. Then the true purpose of the Law would be realized by every man, namely, that man would be lead into a fruitful and abundant life flowing out of an inner relationship with God. It was this type of relationship that was prophesied of, and modelled, by Jesus,

> 'Then I said, *"Behold, I come; In the scroll of the book it is written of me. I delight to do Your will, O my God, And your law is within my heart."'*
>
> Psalm 40:7-8

Once our spirit has been renewed, God's primary channel of instruction is the human heart. Fellowship with Him moves from a strict outward observance to an inward relationship. It was this that allowed David to eat the shewbread (1), Elijah to be fed by ravens (2), permitted the disciples to pluck the heads of grain with impunity (3) and it was this that moved Jesus to talk to an adulterous Samaritan woman (4) and heal on the Sabbath (5).

Gideon

The story of Gideon's calling to lead Israel to overcome the Midianites shows God patiently leading him to a deeper level of belief. It starts with the Angel of the LORD coming to him while

---

(1) 1 Samuel 21:4-6. (2) 1 Kings 17:6. (3) Luke 6:1. (4) John 4:17-18.
(5) Luke 6:7; 14:3.

he is threshing grain to hide it from the marauding Midianites (1). The Angel announces, '*the LORD is with you, you mighty man of valor!*' (2). With this announcement comes an awareness of God's presence to challenge the status quo; Gideon is not alone and this new-found partnership means he is in fact a powerful warrior champion of great strength. Heaven is ushering in the future! God is, 'calling things that do not exist as though they did' (3). However, Gideon, based on his earthly perspective, is not yet convinced. He immediately questions the evidence of God's presence and his earthly qualifications. At which point, the LORD interjects by saying,

'*Surely I will be with you, and you shall defeat the Midianites as one man.*'

Judges 6:16

While most commentators interpret this to mean that the enemy is as '*one man*', the full context of this passage, demands otherwise. On a grander scale, any Old Testament suggestion of union with God is a road sign to what would be achieved at Calvary. Ultimately, that, 'One Man', is Christ and no matter what our earthly circumstances dictate, this is a prophetic decree that 'in Christ' all of our adversaries are defeated.

Gideon asks for a sign and makes an offering. The offering is struck by the angel's staff signifying judgment, and fire, a picture of the wrath of God, then consumes it. This episode prefigures the death of Christ upon the cross. Gideon recognizes through the sign performed that he has seen God as we do at the foot of the cross. At this point, Gideon receives an impartation of the peace of God (4). The word 'peace' is the Hebrew, 'Shalom'. While the word can mean the 'absence of strife' the general meaning at its root is 'completion' and 'fulfilment' by entering into a state of wholeness and restored, unimpaired relationship.

(1) Judges 6:11ff. (2) Judges 6:12. (3) Romans 4:17. (4) Judges 6:23.

Though Gideon is now one with God, like a newborn Christian, his experience and knowledge of God does not yet match his position. He may be joined to God, but is still divided within. So when asked to destroy the family idols he does so by night, fearful of retaliation from family and friends (1). The story progresses with the Spirit of the LORD coming upon him (2), but he is still double-minded. He requests a sign that a woollen fleece placed on the threshing floor overnight would receive dew while the ground around it would remain dry (3). When this is performed just as requested, Gideon, still battling within, requests the reverse to happen, namely, that dew would fall on the ground, but not on the fleece. The Lord performs both signs. What does the fleece signify? The first night where the dew falls on the fleece is a prophetic picture of the approval of God on the sacrificed lamb of God (4), at the threshing floor of judgment. The dry ground around it depicts mankind (h) outside the blessing of God. On the third day, (after the second night) that blessing, shown in the dew of heaven, has moved from Christ onto mankind. Through Christ, believers are under an open heaven. However many, like Gideon, do not yet realize it flows through the human spirit.

(h) Man as dust of earth: Adam created from dust: Genesis 2:7; cf. 2 Corinthians 4:7.

The Lord now speaks to Gideon, who by this time has gathered an army of some 32,000 men, and instructs him to give those who are fearful an opportunity to turn from the coming battle (5). Fear causes division between heart and mouth. It is one thing to say we believe, but if we harbor fear in our heart we are a divided man and the enemy readily routs us under pressure. After twenty-two thousand leave the front lines (6), the Lord says to Gideon that his army is still too big for God to get the glory from the victory that awaits them. So He coaches Gideon in how to separate the ones He will use to face the enemy. God tells Gideon to bring them to the water, where,

(1) Judges 6:27. (2) Judges 6:35. (3) Judges 6:36-38. (4) cf Genesis 3:21; Exodus 12:3-14. (5) Judges 7:3. (6) Judges 7:3.

"'Everyone who laps from the water with his tongue, as a dog laps, you shall set apart by himself; likewise everyone who gets down on his knees to drink."

And the number of those who lapped, putting their hand to their mouth, was three hundred men; but all the rest of the people got down on their knees to drink water.'

Judges 7:5-6

God chooses the three hundred men to be the ones He would use to save and deliver Israel. Amongst commentators there are two main lines of thought on why God chooses the three hundred. One group says God chose those who were more alert as displayed by the fact that they did not lose sight of any prospective attack when stooping to drink. This argument doesn't make sense when you consider that God was the one who was going to give the victory, and the very reason He was narrowing the number of men was so Israel could not claim the victory. If He was going to use elite Rangers/SAS troops surely they could claim the victory? The other line of reasoning is that the ones who bowed their knees were those who, in type, bowed to idols, and therefore, God would not use them.

It is one thing to get revelation, it is quite another to apply it.

Hope waits expectantly for revelation, faith is revelation applied, determined faith produces substance.

Neither of these arguments satisfy the context. Those who lift the hand to the mouth and lap like dogs are those who bring the word from their hearts, depicted by the cupped hand, to their mouths (cf chapter 3 note f page 33). That is, their heart and mouth are saying the same thing. Those who kneeled to drink are a picture of those who readily fold when the word is tried within them. This interpretation not only fits with God's previous thinning of the army, by weeding out the fearful but is also confirmed by the actual 'battle'. However, Gideon is still carrying fear in his heart, so God instructs him to go down to the edge of the enemy's camp with his servant, Purah (1) (i),

(i) Purah: (H6513) Branch (cf. Isaiah 11:1; Jeremiah 23:5; 33:15; Zechariah 3:8; 6:12).

(1) Judges 7:10.

49

where he hears two men talking about a dream. When he hears the interpretation his heart is strengthened and he is now ready as, 'one man' (having his heart and head in alignment), to send the enemy packing. The 'substance' that changed his outlook wasn't outward things like the size of the army, or their fighting prowess, it was a dream, a revelation within, that was the foundation of his faith. Up until this time Israel was 'impoverished' (1) by the enemy, but that was about to change.

The three hundred men came to the edge of the enemy's camp carrying a torch covered with an earthen vessel in the left hand, and a ram's horn trumpet in the right hand (j). Just as there is a changing of the guard in the enemy's camp at midnight, '*they blew the trumpets and broke the pitchers that were in their hands*' (2). And they cried, '*The sword of the LORD and of Gideon*' (3)! The left hand is associated with the heart and the right hand the mouth. So what is depicted here when the pitchers are broken is that earthly constraints are broken off so that the glory of God within can truly shine forth. The trumpets symbolise the voice of God being decreed from the mouth (k). This is confirmed by what Gideon and his men cry out, '*The sword of the LORD and of Gideon!*' Those familiar with the New Testament will quickly realize that the sword is a picture of the word (4). '*The sword of the LORD*' is God's word in the heart, and the sword, '*of Gideon*' is that same word in his mouth (l). Gideon got the victory in his heart through overhearing a dream and broke off earthly limitations by lining up his words with what had been deposited in his heart. The glory of God was displayed and the enemy were defeated (m)!

Overcoming Fear

The story of Gideon emphasises how fear is a major obstacle to those wanting to receive the promises of God (n). As we have

(j) Shofar: see note (a) chapter 12 page 158.

(k) Trumpet as a voice: Exodus 19:16,19; Isaiah 58:1; Revelation 1:10; 4:1.

(l) The two in alignment constitutes one man: Jesus Christ Judges 6:16.

(m) 300 as The glory of God: Genesis 5:22; 1 Kings 10:17.

(n) The Promised Land can also equate to living in the promises of God; cf. Hebrews 11:9.

(1) Judges 6:6. (2) Judges 7:19. (3) Judges 7:20. (4) Hebrews 4:12.

seen, fear divides, so that the heart and head are not saying the same thing. It is not surprising, then, that when God was addressing Joshua prior to entering the Promised Land, He encourages him not to be fearful,

> *'Have I not commanded you? Be strong and of a good courage; be not afraid, neither be dismayed, for the Lord your God is with you wherever you go.'*

Joshua 1:9

Further to this, throughout Israel's journey from Egypt to the Promised Land God names seven nations that they will face and overcome in possessing Canaan (1). However, when God addresses Joshua to prepare him to bring Israel into Canaan He only names the Hittites as the nation they need to oust. It is not without purpose that He does so. The root of the word, 'Hittite' is 'to be afrighted by fear'! A person whose spirit is in fear will not hold onto a promise given to meet his need. He will, at best, vacillate between belief and unbelief (2), and like Gideon's 'knee bending' troops he will buckle under pressure.

It is also interesting that Joshua's charge is to 'divide' the inheritance of the Promised Land amongst the nation of Israel (3). The sons of God are privileged to divide the spoils of the promises of God, IF they are not first divided by fear. As my friend Chris Blackeby, says, 'All fear is fear of death!' Just as fear of sickness and disease is ultimately a fear of death, so fear of not finding a life partner and fear of divorce is death to marriage; fear of giving is death to financial freedom and the fear of rejection is death to acceptance, and so on. Just as Joshua had to cross over Jordan (o), to step into heaven and partake of the promises of God, we have to traverse death (in Him) and all its associated fears. All fear is overcome by an awareness of His perfect love, which is cultivated by relationship in His presence.

(o) The name Jordan means 'Descender' or 'Death'.

(1) Exodus 3:8, 17; 23:23; 33:2; 34:11; Deuteronomy 7:1; 20:17. (2) James 1:6. (3) Joshua 1:6.

This is why in the verse above God says to Joshua, '*I will be with you wherever you go*'. His union with Joshua is witness to that love. This is the reason the Apostle John writes, '*...perfect love casts out fear*' (1), and is behind Jesus' request of the Father,

> '*...that they may be made <u>perfect in one</u>, and that the world may know that You have sent Me, and have loved them as You have loved me.*'

John 17:23

How will the world know Jesus is the Messiah, who has taken away man's sin so that they can now move into relationship with the Father? They will know when their attention is caught by the supernatural manifestations that surround the sons of God who have overcome fear - in Him - and are moving in perfect love!

Man. Utd. Vs Sunderland

'I saw a football match between Manchester United and Sunderland which ended in a 1-1 draw, Sunderland scored through Asamoah Gyan in the 2nd minute while Man. Utd. equalised through Sun Park in the 53rd minute.'

To come back to the dream at the beginning of the chapter, we see that God is using the dreamer's interest in football (or soccer in the USA) to describe the battle he is experiencing within. Manchester United which is commonly abbreviated, 'Man. Utd.', refers to the 'one man' having the heart and head saying the same thing. Whereas Sunderland describes someone as the 'land' (an earthen vessel) who has been 'sundered' or divided. The dream, then, shows that his heart was not in his belief and he was losing ground to the enemy. He may even have taken a break from God, because things didn't seem to

(1) 1 John 4:18.

be working (p). However, after the break he has come out renewed, with Jesus enthroned in his heart (q) and equalised. The fact that there is still 37 minutes (r) of play remaining after the second goal suggests that the dreamer needs to continue to seek God's presence, where he will move from a draw into victory!

(p) A game of football is 90 minutes, with a half time break at 45 minutes.

(q) Sun Park cf. Malachi 4:2. NB that a park is a place of rest and relaxation.

(r) Thirty-seven is the right time to reign in rest. See side note (e) page 135.

Prayer:

Father, I realize that much of my prayer life has been asking You to bless what I initiate. I now see that the word of truth has spiritual impact when I align my mouth with it. Please remove any root of fear in me and all double-mindedness. Please give fresh deposits of revelation to my heart, and by faith I will speak agreement with them. Amen.

Summary:

- Heart and mouth alignment is needed for spiritual salvation, which includes healing and deliverance.
- Truth, is the unveiled reality lying at the basis of, and agreeing with, an appearance.
- A double-minded man is one whose heart and mouth do not align.
- At a fundamental level, meditation on the law is contemplation and muttering the word which comes from His presence, like the rain of heaven, or as an arrow to the heart.
- It was promised that the new covenant was going to be imparted to the inner man and flow outward.
- Fear causes division between the heart and mouth.
- The story of Gideon depicts the double-minded believer becoming unified.
- Revelation to the heart is the foundation of faith.
- The glory of God is displayed when we line our mouths with God's word in our heart and break off earthly constraints.
- God's union with us is witness of His love.
- All fear is overcome by an awareness of His perfect love, which is cultivated by relationship in His presence.

Chapter 5

The Making of a Warrior

**His Presence
the Place of Strength**

*"I urge you to pray less, and listen more...
for when you listen, you will know exactly what to pray...."*
William Penn

Much of what comes through the mouth in prayer is, at best, ineffective because it does not come from the heart. The above admonition by William Penn to 'listen more' before opening the doors of one's lips before God, is as appropriate today, as in the day it was written. And probably more so given the current busyness of everyday life. Too often the head charges off with its own ideas without consultation with the heart, and the result, is powerless prayer. We have all experienced someone obsessively filling every moment of time with the sound of their own voice, either preaching or in prayer, only to have another person hit the spot, with but a few words. It is not so much the length of a discourse, its volume, or how dynamic the presentation, that matters. I have seen people respond 'en masse' even to a monotone presentation because God spoke to their hearts. The key, of course, is hearing from God, and then speaking on His behalf.

Martha and Mary

When Martha was distracted by much serving, while Mary sat at Jesus' feet listening attentively, Jesus responded to Martha's plea for help from her sister by saying,

'Martha, Martha, you are worried and troubled about many things. But <u>one thing</u> is needed, and Mary has chosen that <u>good part</u>, which will <u>not</u> be <u>taken away</u> from her.'

Luke 10:41-42 (Emphasis added)

His words capture for us three critical truths. Firstly, that in the midst of life's hustle the 'one thing' above all others that is needed is time at His feet. Such time sensitizes the listener to Heaven. It was Mary, who later recognized the Glory of God (1) and prophetically anointed Jesus for His burial (2) (a).

(a) Mary, in contrast to other followers of Christ, who were still focusing on the pages of this world (John 11:37, 46; 12:5-6).

Next, note that Jesus says what Mary was receiving *'will not be taken away'* from her. Only eternal things cannot be taken from us. While Mary was sitting listening to Jesus she was imbibing manna from heaven - that which comes from beyond this world - and was imbued with the very Life of God itself. It is this Living word that does not *'fall to the ground'* (3)

(1) 2 Corinthians 4:6. (2) John 12:5-7. (3) 1 Samuel 3:19.

but penetrates hearts.

Finally, Jesus describes Mary's deposit as *'good'*. The Greek word used here is, 'Agathos' which describes something benevolent, a thing of quality (b), a quality deposit that is outright beneficial to others. Wow! On many occasions sitting at Jesus' feet is actually more beneficial to others than meeting their immediate needs (c). That is because it is not the quantity or the intensity of our words, but the quality - a *'word in season'* - that matters (1). Without doubt, it was a sensitivity born in the presence of His Father that caused Jesus to respond to the question on Nicodemus' heart before he had asked it (2), choose to minister to only one man at the pool of Bethesda (3) and delay in coming to Lazarus (4).

(b) There is another Greek word 'Kalos' (G2570) that means good, which describes something of 'harmony', but Jesus deliberately avoids this word and chooses instead to use a word 'Agathos' (G0018) that means a quality deposit that is beneficial to others.

(c) Mary was being more productive than Martha.

One time, with my good friend Adam F. Thompson, on our return flight to Australia after an intense period of ministry. We were unwinding, watching a movie or two. I chose to watch, 'The Karate Kid'. When the movies had finished, Adam said to me, 'Why did you watch that?' I said, 'I watched that for one line, where Mister Miyagi says to his apprentice, '"Being still' and 'doing nothing' are not the same thing!'" Both Martha and Mister Miyagi's student, were receiving the same lesson. Things are not always as they seem outwardly, there are two realms and it is the eternal one that has priority.

Strong and Courageous

Having previously considered both the importance of meditation and revelation in Joshua's instructions for success in Canaan, another major key is provided in Joshua's opening chapter. The phrase, *'Be strong and courageous'* is used four times (5). If God is going to repeat Himself with such fervency in a single chapter then there must be something important in what He is saying. Let us first consider the word, *'Courageous'*.

(1) Isaiah 50:4. (2) John 3:2-3. (3) John 5:3-6. (4) John 11:6. (5) Joshua 1:6, 7, 9, 18; cf Deuteronomy 31:23.

In the Book of Ruth, the same word is translated, '*Determined*'. The setting for its use is after the death of Naomi's husband and sons, when she is returning to Judah with her two daughters-in-law. As the trio sets out, Naomi puts forth the natural reasons why the pair of widows should not come with her. One of them, Orpah, turns back, but Ruth displays her resolve to go with Naomi by vehemently declaring nothing but death could prevent her from making the journey (1). At that point, the scripture says of Naomi,

> '*When she saw that she was <u>determined</u> to go with her, she stopped speaking to her.*'

Ruth 1:18 (Emphasis added)

The word, '*Determined*' here is the same Hebrew word as that translated '*Courageous*' in Joshua. The context provided by Ruth and the fact that she was willing to lay her life down helps us appreciate the gritty determination that God was instilling in Joshua as he faced the task of ousting the inhabitants of Canaan.

When God uses the word, 'Strength' in the command to be, '*Strong and courageous,*' He is not primarily talking about physical strength, even though physical muscle and stamina would be required to complete the task ahead. To see what God is saying here we need to look further afield.

Apprehending what God is saying here requires knowledge of broader cultural and contextual applications. Referring to the life of Abraham, the father of faith, provides insight into the concept of spiritual strength. Talking about Abraham, the Apostle Paul, succinctly captures the secret of his faith, when he states,

> '*As it is written, I have made you a father of many nations,*

---

(1) Ruth 1:14, 16-17.

Before Him whom he believed! even God, who quickens the dead, and calls those things which be not as though they were. Who against hope believed in hope, that he might become the father of many nations, according to that which was spoken, So shall your seed be.

And not being weak in faith, he considered not his own body now dead, when he was about a hundred years old, neither yet the deadness of Sarah's womb: He staggered not at the promise of God through unbelief; but was strong in faith, giving glory to God; And being fully persuaded that, what He had promised, He was able also to perform. And therefore it was imputed to him for righteousness.'

Romans 4:17-22 (KJV Modernized, Emphasis added)

Paul reveals not only that Abraham was strong in faith, but how he gained his strength. Abraham's strength came, '*before Him whom he believed*' and '*according to that which was spoken*'. In other words, Abraham was in the presence of God when he received a promise from God, and that word of promise to his heart provided a footing for his faith. This is the unwritten message emphasised by David the Psalmist,

> *Wait on the Lord: be of good courage,*
> *and he shall strengthen thine heart:*
> *wait, I say, on the Lord.'*

Psalm 27:14 (KJV)

And in another place, one of the most well-known verses in the Bible reiterates David,

> '*But they that wait upon the Lord shall renew their strength;*
> *they shall mount up with wings as eagles;*
> *they shall run, and not be weary; and they shall walk,*

and not faint.'

Isaiah 40:31 (KJV)

It is the rhema word spoken to the heart that is the basis of strong faith. In Christ, we have an ever-open door of entry to wait upon the Father, where we are able to access the promises of God. Whatever we receive in that place before Him, we have His assurance of receiving, because scripture records,

'All the promises of God in Him are Yes, and in Him Amen, to the glory of God.'

2 Corinthians 1:20

The 'Amen' is the privilege that believers have in speaking the promise into manifestation. Just as Gideon and his 300 men revealed the torches concealed by the earthen vessels and took the shofar to their lips, so we are privileged to reveal God's glory by aligning our mouths with the promise He has placed within.

Gird up the Loins

To take this further requires an excursion into Eastern cultural thinking. When the expression *'gird up the loins'* is used in scripture it describes the process of tucking one's tunic into the belt around the waist in preparation either for a journey or for war.

(d) The staff is a picture of the word he carried: (cf. Exodus 14:16 and Hebrews 4:12). There is a measure of interchangeability between rod and staff. However, compare Psalm 23:4; where 'rod' may be understood as a reference to discipline/authority, while 'staff' to nurture/protection/support. Moses lifted the rod, Gehazi carried the staff.

With the loins girded: the Passover lamb was eaten (1), Israel rose up against her enemies (2), Elijah outran Ahab's chariot (3), Gehazi was commissioned to carry the word (d), to resurrect the Shunammite's son (4), Elisha sent a prophet to anoint Jehu as king (5) and Job was prepared like a warrior to face God's questioning (6).

(1) Exodus 12:11. (2) Deuteronomy 1:41. (3) 1 Kings 18:46. (4) 2 Kings 4:29. (5) 2 Kings 9:1. (6) Job 38:3.

The loins speak of more than our physical private parts. The loins are representative of man's strength, physically they are the waist and hips. For example, Jacob had his hip put out of joint because he was no longer to lean on his own strength, but on God's (1). Figuratively, the loins speak of the source of strength, human virility and they represent the masculine virtue of acting like a warrior. That this refers not just to men only is proven by its use in the description of the virtuous wife (2).

The Apostle Peter in the New Testament uses this imagery when he exhorts us as believers to, *'gird up the loins of your mind...'* (3). Girding up the loins of one's mind is not merely gathering up the loose thoughts, it is gathering up the loose thoughts that would otherwise make one trip, with the emphasis of centering them around the deposit placed in the heart! Each of the examples of girded loins described above, reveal people carrying such a deposit.

It is also important to realize that the 'mind of Christ' is not so much a rational deposit to the brain, it is the spiritual download to the heart (4). That a reference to the 'mind' may speak of one's heart is shown in Paul's writings to the Roman church, when he says,

> *'That you may with <u>one mind</u> and <u>one mouth</u> glorify God, even the Father of our Lord Jesus Christ.'*
>
> Romans 15:6 (KJV Modernized, Emphasis added)

With these two elements - mind and mouth - culminating in the glorification of God, this passage clearly parallels the model presented by Gideon's encased torch and trumpet and Paul's earlier reference to receiving the promises of God by a double affirmation, 'yes' and 'amen' (5).

The repeated call upon Joshua to be *'strong and courageous'*,

---

(1) Genesis 32:25. (2) Proverbs 31:17. (3) 1 Peter 1:13. (4) 1 Corinthians. 2:16. (5) 2 Corinthians 1:20.

is then, a command to wait before God to receive His word. This word, regardless of the observable facts and opposition, is to be the foundational strength for the taking of the Promised Land. It is effectively, 'the receipt of the promise' (1). When we muster a determination based on the word placed in our hearts, it is like, 'a hand stuck to a sword', and it is that which displaces the enemy (2).

The Weapons of Our Warfare

As the New Testament points out, our battle is not, '*against flesh and blood*', but against, '*spiritual hosts of wickedness in heavenly places*' (3). That said, to defeat a spiritual foe we need spiritual weapons. The foundation of all spiritual weaponry is the word of God in our hearts, or as Paul puts it in outlining the Armor of God, '*Stand therefore, having girded your waist with truth...*' (4). In this passage Paul is referring to having our hearts living in the landscape of the kingdom fed by the written word of God. However, in that place he anticipates more: quickened scriptures, revelation, prophetic words, dreams and visions to enable us to go on the offensive with '*...the sword of the Spirit, which is the word (rhema) of God,*' (5)

In this vein, he commands Timothy to wage war according to the prophecies that have been given him.

'This charge I commit to you, son Timothy, according to the prophecies previously made concerning you, that by them you may wage the good warfare.'

1 Timothy 1:18

Now a 'charge' is a command not an option. It is a 'must do'. Every believer has times when he needs to pull out the list of prophecies, dreams, visions and quickened scriptures and 'strengthen' himself by supplanting all opposition with the

---

(1) Hebrews 9:15. (2) 2 Samuel 23:10. (3) Ephesians 6:12. (4) Ephesians 6:14. (5) Ephesians 6:17.

promises of God. In that place, it is critically important what comes out of our mouths. Like Joshua's men circling Jericho we are charged that, 'no word shall proceed out of your mouth' (1). That is, no word that is contrary to what God has said should be released into the spirit realm to disempower the promises of God. This is, effectively, drawing up the garments of our loose thoughts around our hearts because we are in warfare.

Tongues

It can be argued that the sound coming from the trumpets in the mouths of Joshua's priests is the Old Testament equivalent of speaking in tongues. How? The Book of Revelation tells us that the trumpet is a *'voice'* (2). Also, in choosing a metaphor to describe speaking in tongues without an interpretation, Paul the Apostle, says,

'For if the trumpet makes an uncertain sound, who will prepare for battle?'

1 Corinthians 14: 8

Further to this, the Bible records that when the Spirit came upon Gideon, he blew a trumpet (3). Then, when he led 300 men to defeat the Midianites with trumpets in their mouths he cried out, *'The sword of the LORD, and of Gideon'* (4). You don't have to be a rocket scientist to realize that the trumpet in their mouths symbolised the sword of the Spirit (5).

At another time when rebuilding the walls of Jerusalem, Nehemiah describes the setting by saying,

'Every one of the builders had his sword girded at his side as he built. And the one who sounded the trumpet was beside me."

Nehemiah 4:18

(1) Joshua 6:10. (2) Revelation 4:1; cf. Exodus 19:16, 19. (3) Judges 6:34. (4) Judges 7:20. (5) Ephesians 6:17.

(e) Jubilee is the year of God's favor and is marked by trumpets. The Hebrew word 'yobhel' is the shortened 'qeren ha-yobhel', meaning the horn of a ram. The horn was made into a trumpet, and thus the word 'yobhel' came to be used as a synonym of trumpet. In Leviticus 25:9 a loud trumpet was to proclaim liberty throughout the country on the 10th day of the 7th month (the Day of Atonement), after the lapse of 7 sabbaths of years = 49 years. Thus, every 50th year was to be announced as a jubilee year. All real property was to automatically revert to its original owner (Leviticus 25:10 ; cf. 25:13), and those who, compelled by poverty, had sold themselves as slaves to their brothers, should regain their liberty (Leviticus 25:10 ; cf. 25:39).

(f) The subject of speaking in tongues is covered more comprehensively in chapter 12.

Viewed through spiritual eyes this scene describes the builders as those with the word in their hearts, seen here as a sword girded at their sides. The one who sounded the trumpet is a reference to the Holy Spirit because later Nehemiah explains, *'Wherever you hear the sound of the trumpet...Our God will fight for us'* (1). Finally, considering that, *'where the Spirit of the Lord is, there is liberty'* (2), it should come as no surprise that the Year of Liberty - Jubilee - is marked by the blowing of trumpets (e).

In emulating Joshua's men in overcoming enemy strongholds that we face, speaking or singing in tongues is a powerful weapon that releases the Spirit of God to fight on our behalf (f).

'When you go to war in your land against the enemy who oppresses you, then you shall sound an alarm with the trumpets, and you will be remembered before the LORD your God, and you will be saved from your enemies.'

Numbers 10:9

Going Out and Coming In

After defeating Goliath, it is recorded that David went 'out' and came 'in' before the people (3). The terms - out and in - are a reference to his leading King Saul's men out to battle and returning to the city in triumph. When Solomon came to the throne he openly acknowledged his inability to go out and in,

'Now, O Lord my God, You have made Your servant king instead of my father David, but I am but a little child; I do not know how to go out or come in.

And Your servant is in the midst of Your people....'

1 Kings 3:7-8

(1) Nehemiah 4:20. (2) 2 Corinthians.3:17. (3) 1 Samuel 18:13, 16.

It is interesting that God responded to his request by granting him wisdom and understanding (1). We might view these endowments as being associated more with the heart than with warfare, unless we recognize that the basis of David's fighting prowess was his relationship with God. Before David went to battle he would come before God (2). It was the instruction and strategies he received from God that made him a successful warrior.

May I suggest that where the text reports David going out and in to battle before the people, his relationship with God is being hinted at. This is because the precedent for going out and coming in, as an act of worship, had already been established by Moses, who went 'out' from the camp and went 'in' to the tabernacle (3).

That said, success in any field of human endeavor is similarly undergirded by our response to Jesus' invitation to go in and come out to do the work of the Father (chapter 2 page 19). The stable-footed warrior is he who enters 'in' to hear from God and comes 'out' to apply what he hears (4) (g) (h).

Counterpunch in the Opposite Spirit

Having previously outlined that heaven is '*the world to come*', it is time to mention another verse that builds on that theme,

'For He has not put the world to come, of which we speak, in subjection to angels.'

Hebrews 2:5

In outlining that '*the world to come*' is not subject to angels, this verse infers that heaven is in subjection to us (in Christ). I say this because sometimes our revelation through the Spirit is

Entering heaven is as much about leaving earth.

- Shut the door (Matthew 6:6)
- Moses (Exodus 33:7-8)
- Jesus (Mark 1:35; Acts 1:21)
cf. James 4:8.

(g) Does going in and out suggest you cannot be in continuous unbroken communion with God all the time? We are both in constant communion with God and this realm at the same time for He has declared He will never leave us (Matthew 28:20; Hebrews 13:5). However, because the reality is that the rigours of life on earth demand predominantly conscious interaction from us, our spirit man has to be developed to 'tap' into the eternal realm. Going out of the camp of this world and into the tabernacle of His presence is the primary means to develop this spiritual sensitivity.

(h) See page 66.

(1) 1 Kings 3:12. (2) 2 Samuel 5:19, 23. (3) Exodus 33:8. (4) cf. Acts 1:21.

(h) There are proponents of mystical union who claim to live in the secret place of God's presence, but such assertions are prone to inactivity. The scriptural examples discussed here paint a different story. The fact that John writes, *'I was in the Spirit on the Lord's day...'* (Revelation 1:10) suggests that he was not always in that place! True mysticism is a going 'in' to hear and a coming 'out' to apply what was heard.

Daniel had three quiet times a day because the time between was the maximum he could go without being in His presence! Daniel 6:10,13.

of a negative nature. For example, we may have a dream with a negative outcome such as sickness, death, divorce, loss of work or a church split in it. Dreams or insights like this can be understood as the Spirit of God revealing the enemy's plans. What do you do in these situations? What is called for is not agreement with the enemy's plans for sickness, death, a church split, etc. but a counterpunch in the opposite Spirit. At this point it is vital to understand our authority in the spirit realm. In these type of scenarios a proclamation or decree of healing, wholeness or love needs to be released into the situation.

Prayer:

Father, develop a heart in me that loves to wait in Your presence. I desire to be like Mary, so that I may receive a deposit that cannot be taken away from me and that is beneficial to others. Help me to balance my 'doing' with my 'being' in Your presence as a strong stable-footed warrior who goes 'in' to hear Your voice and comes 'out' to apply what I have heard. Amen.

Summary:

- Listen first before opening your mouth in the presence of God.

- There are two realms and the eternal one has priority.

- God's word to our heart gives us strength.

- Determination is a twin sister to faith to see the promises of God manifest.

- Girding up the loins of one's mind is not merely gathering up loose thoughts, it is gathering up the loose thoughts that would otherwise make one trip, and centering them around the deposit placed in our heart.

- The mind of Christ is not a rational thought but rather a spiritual download to the heart.

- To defeat a spiritual foe requires spiritual weapons.

- The use of trumpets can be shown to be one Old Testament equivalent of speaking in tongues in the New.

- The stable-footed warrior is he who enters 'in' to hear from God and comes 'out' to apply what he hears.

- Recognizing our authority, we are at times called upon to counterpunch in the opposite spirit to thwart the plans of the enemy.

Chapter 6

Authority

Heaven Rules OK!

Picture the scene, it is the mid 1500's, a time when any religious disagreement with the crown brought either an axeman's blade down on one's neck or burning at the stake. John Knox, Scottish reformer, was summoned to court. On his way in he was warned that Catholic Queen Mary was in a foul mood. Without breaking stride, Knox kept walking, replying, 'Why should I be afraid of a queen when I have just spent three hours with God?'

This story highlights that we live under two coexistent authority structures, the seen and unseen, the earthly and heavenly. It also answers the question, 'Which of the two carries more clout?' This dynamic is scripturally illustrated when Nebuchadnezzar, the king of Babylon, has a dream in which angels come and chop down a tree that is providing shelter. The dream was a warning that the moment the earthly king forgot who it was that really placed him in power, would be the same instant when it would be taken from him. In interpreting the dream Daniel also explains its purpose, which was,

'...that the living may know that the Most High rules in the kingdom of men, Gives it to whomever He will, and sets up over it the lowest of men.'

Daniel 4:17

On a similar note, when Jesus was on trial before Pontius Pilate, He declared that it was God who was over the affairs of men.

'Then said Pilate to Him, "Are You not speaking to me? Do You not know that I have power to crucify You, and have power to release You?" Jesus answered, "You could have no power at all against Me, unless it had been given you from above."'

John 19:10-11

Finally, on this point, in the interchange between Jesus and the Centurion seeking healing for his servant, the Gentile soldier states that he is also, *'a man under authority'*. In making that statement he is not only acknowledging that all power is disseminated from above, but in requesting Christ's assistance, is also declaring which is superior.

So there are two coexistent realms and the spiritual has preeminence over the earthly. It is clear that the Centurion understood the distinction between the two. In requesting that Jesus not come under his roof, he was saying, 'There is no need for You to come under my covering', which as a reference to an area of his personal jurisdiction, also declared his recognition of Jesus' superior influence. The Centurion said,

> '...“Lord, I am not worthy that You should come under my roof. But only speak a word, and my servant will be healed.
>
> For I also am a man under authority, having soldiers under me. And I say to this one, 'Go,' and he goes; and to another, 'Come,' and he comes; and to my servant, 'Do this,' and he does it.”
>
> When Jesus heard it, He marveled, and said to those who followed, “Assuredly, I say to you, I have not found such great faith, not even in Israel!”'

Matthew 8:8-10

The Centurion's comments and Jesus response make it clear that in both kingdoms authority is administered by words. This is critically important. Remember the childhood ditty, 'Bricks and stones may break my bones, but words will never hurt me.' The reality is nothing could be further from the truth. Words, and particularly rhema words are the most powerful creative instruments in the universe! The rhema word is the spoken word, or the living voice of God. The Bible says, *'Faith comes by hearing, and hearing by the word (rhema) of God'* (1). It is the rhema word and not the 'logos' or written word that strengthens the heart with faith. When the Bible speaks of, *'the sword of the Spirit, which is the word of God'*, it is talking about the rhema word. Therefore, it is the rhema word that we use when we go on the offensive against the enemy.

Now it is also important to understand that God can speak the rhema word using means beyond mere spoken language. The rhema word can be received through a gesture, a dream, a

(1) Romans 10:17.

71

vision, an enactment, a quickened scripture, a prophecy (a). It may come as a voice within a voice or any other multitude of ways. In fact, God will speak to you in whatever way you listen.

When Elijah threw his mantle over Elisha, God was speaking though not a word was spoken. When Jeremiah visited the potter, when Ezekiel dug through a wall, when Jesus fed 5000 people, or caused 153 fish to be caught, God was speaking.

At one time I was about to minister in a church in Wollongong, Australia. The room was a hive of activity as musicians, ushers and helpers were setting up. I needed time alone with God, so I made my way out and found a path that led around the side of the building. I sat on a modular brick wall and shut my eyes and acknowledged to God my total need of Him. When I opened my eyes I noticed a dead bee lying upside down right in the middle of the path before me. I shut my eyes again and continued in prayer, but when I opened them again I saw it wasn't actually a bee, but a big black fly. It was on its back and the wings were at right angles to the body. It looked, 'deader than dead' because of the angle of the wings. The thought came to me, what is a fly representative of in scripture? Well, the devil is called, 'the lord of the flies' (1). So a fly is a demon or evil spirit. I thought, are You going to kill a spirit here tonight Lord? As spirits don't die, was He going to cast out a demon? I said out loud, 'Don't get carried away here Adrian, but if You want to do that, Lord, Hallelujah!' Two hours or so later I was praying for those who came forward. To be honest, I had totally forgotten about the fly encounter. I came to a woman who fell to the floor as I began to pray. I thought, either I am really anointed here tonight, or that was too easy. I took the second option and decided to come against the 'torment' that was over her life. When she screamed the whole place reverberated. After she had been set free I moved on and completed praying for other

Rhema and Logos

(a) This is not to deny that meditating on the written word (Logos) is also a proven avenue for receiving the spoken word (Rhema). However, this volume deliberately emphasises additional methods to broaden this base for hearing the voice of God.

(1) Matthew 12:24.

needs in the prayer line. It wasn't until I stepped into the car to leave that I realized that God had spoken to me earlier through that fly, of what was about to happen.

Elijah throwing his mantle over Elisha was a word, though no words were spoken. If you are aware of the story, you will know that at a later date Elisha used that mantle to divide the River Jordan (1). In the New Testament we are told that the word of God is the instrument used to divide (2). So Elisha is figuratively given Elijah's mantle, without a spoken word, and then when he has spiritually grown into it he uses it to divide the Jordan. The mantle was the word of God! Elisha was wearing God's word.

This not only has past application in scripture, but also ramifications for us today. We can wear words. A woman asked me during a conference about a recent dream she had. In the dream she saw a snake on her wrist and was concerned about it. When I asked her what she did as a profession, she related that she was a masseuse or remedial therapist. I asked whether she utilised any New Age teaching in her practice and she responded that she had been Christian for more than 20 years and had long since rid her consultancy of all such materials. I said, "In that case, we needed more time to allow God to show us the meaning of the dream". That night I was awakened by a vision of a 'Medic Alert' bracelet on someone's wrist and knew because of the snake representation on these bracelets that it was the answer to her dream. The next day I asked her whether she had a Medic Alert bracelet. She said she did, but that she didn't wear it. I knew now what the dream meant. The dream was showing her that she was wearing words that a professional had pronounced over her! We wear words, particularly, those that come from

Who Am I?

*I commenced my ministry defeating a formidable foe
I defeated the enemy with the 'words of a servant'
I cried 'I thirst!'
I was betrayed by my own people
My love was misunderstood
I was anointed with the 7 Spirits of God
It is recorded that I died twice*

Answer: Chapter 10.

(1) 2 Kings 2:14. (2) Hebrews 4:12.

authority figures or people we hold in high regard. We need to be careful not to wear everything that people say about us. We need to wear only what God says about us because heaven has precedence over earth.

Returning to the interaction between Jesus and the Centurion, the next observation we can make from it is that to wield authority one has to be under authority. Many like to interpret this as being yielded to the local church as the first level of authority. However, our first level of authority is obedience to the word of God. Let me be clear here, there is a need for accountability within the church. In this way the local church provides a measure of safety, nevertheless, our foundational authority is the word of God. Jesus would not have fulfilled His mission if His primary covering was the Pharisees! On the other hand, there is no excuse for someone who is offended with leadership to do things in a wrong and independent spirit. That is called, 'sedition' (b). It was what Absalom did to his father, David, and it was recognized as the sin that brought down Jerusalem (1).

(b) Sedition: incitement of discontent or rebellion against an authority; any action, particularly in speech or writing, promoting such discontent or rebellion.

Without obedience to the word of God there is no authority. If we are not applying what we profess then we don't really believe it, and if we don't believe what we say, then there is no foundation in our heart (2). Any word that comes out of us without a foundation falls to the ground having no base for propulsion. It cannot penetrate because when it meets resistance there is no weight of belief behind it. Our words, like those of Jesus, are meant to be Spirit and life (3). If their source is the soul, they will not carry. When Jesus completed the Sermon on the Mount the scripture records,

'And it came to pass, when Jesus had ended these sayings, the people were astonished at his doctrine. For he taught them as

(1) Ezra 4:15, 19. (2) Matthew 7:26. (3) John 6:63.

74

one having authority, and not as the scribes.'

Matthew 7:28-29 (KJV)

The scribes and Pharisees said one thing but did another (1), therefore they carried no spiritual authority. Another way of saying that is that their words had no spiritual weight behind them. This is why, earlier in that discourse, Jesus taught on this very subject, saying,

'Whoever therefore breaks one of the least of these commandments, and teaches men so, shall be called least in the kingdom of heaven; but whoever does and teaches them, he shall be called great in the kingdom of heaven.

For I say to you, that unless your righteousness exceeds the righteousness of the scribes and Pharisees, you will by no means enter the kingdom of heaven.'

Matthew 5:19-20

A broken commandment is a word with no heart or application behind it. To break the word and teach men so, is to impart a double standard. In this passage Jesus also teaches about righteousness. In using the scribes and Pharisees as His example, He says righteousness is not

(c)	Is righteousness imputed by faith Or the outworking of faith? Answer: Yes (it is both).	
	Faith's acquisition (Imputed by faith)	Faith's application (Obedience / doing)
	Romans 3:22; 4:6; 10:3. 1 Corinthians 1:30. 2 Corinthians 5:21. Phillipians 3:9. James 2:23.	Matthew 5:19-20. Romans 6:13. 1 Timothy 6:11. 2 Timothy 3:16. 1 John 2:29; 3:7, 10.

merely having an intellectual knowledge of the word, but it is also believing and applying it in one's heart (c).

Men and women of stature in the kingdom, who are spoken of here as those who are 'great', are the ones who do what they

(1) Matthew 23:2-3.

say and therefore carry authority. It is that authority that allows them to partake of heaven's provision, or as it is described here, *'enter the kingdom'*. While those who are described as, *'least'* in the kingdom are unable to enter because they profess one thing and do another so that their words carry no spiritual authority.

By way of illustration, I knew a youth pastor, who was called upon to assist in a deliverance. The person leading the deliverance commanded the demon to leave, saying, 'We, as Christians here, demand you leave this person!' The demon replied, 'Who is Christian? This guy is sleeping with his girlfriend!' The would-be pastor found himself doing some very quick repenting.

Now it should be no surprise why Jesus commanded us to, *'Seek first the kingdom of God and His righteousness'* (1). It addresses the reality of the two kingdoms, and recognizes heaven's superiority. It also reinforces the need to understand His level of righteousness, with our hearts fully handed over, so that we be in the place to receive all that He has for us.

The final lesson from the episode with the Centurion is that the servant carries the same authority as the one who sent him. As we are not familiar with kings and their courts this concept is not really fully apprehended today, and because of this the word carried by God's agent does not always take root in the heart of those who need to receive it. The Centurion simply asked Jesus to, *'...only speak a word, and my servant will be healed.'* His request showed He understood that when Jesus spoke it was as God speaking and hence he had faith to receive that which would normally be beyond natural reach.

Similarly, when Martha and Mary 'sent' to Jesus because their brother was sick, Jesus responded that Lazarus' sickness wasn't, *'unto death, but for the glory of God'* (2). Martha

(1) Matthew 6:33. (2) John 11:3-4.

and Mary did not personally go to Jesus, they sent a servant or friend to carry their word to Jesus. Likewise, Jesus did not immediately go to Lazarus' aid. He sent back His response through the same servant who had carried the sister's request for help. His delay in physically coming is why they greeted Him in anguish after their brother's death. When He eventually had arrived at Bethany, Jesus requested that Martha have the stone that covered the grave removed. Martha protested saying there would be a stench. However, Jesus repeated His earlier word by saying, *'Didn't I say to you, that if you would believe, you would see the glory of God?'* (1). When did Jesus say this? He said it the moment it left His lips. It was then carried in the heart of the servant, until, it was delivered to Martha and Mary. The point being, the word carried by the servant was exactly the same as Jesus speaking.

Jesus Himself acknowledged, as the Servant of the Father, that it wasn't about Him, but that He was simply the vessel of the Father, when He said, *'... He that believes on me, believes not on Me, but on Him that sent Me,'* (2).

Jesus was ministering with authority as a servant who heard the word of His Master and went about discharging His duties. This understanding gives us yet another view of Jesus' statements,

'We speak what we know and testify what we have seen....'

John 3:11

'And what He has seen and heard, that He testifies....'

John 3:32

'The words that I speak to you, I do not speak on My own....'

John 14:10

(1) John 11:40. (2) John 12:44 (KJV Modernized).

77

> *'the word which you hear is not Mine but the Father's that sent Me.'*

> John 14:24

And finally,

> *'I speak what I have seen with My Father....'*

> John 8:38

Wow! Doesn't that frame of reference put a new slant on Jesus as the Servant of Jehovah? He wasn't ministering in His own right, but as the Servant of the Father. The Father's authority was displayed in manifestations of power through Him as He delivered the rhema word. Jesus modelled for us that the decrees and utterances of heaven overwrite any earthly script. Oh, how we too, need to present ourselves as vessels, *'fit for the Master's use'* (1), and have *'ears to hear'* the voice of the Spirit of God so that the world may know that He sent us!

(1) 2 Timothy 2:21.

Prayer:

Father, I acknowledge that heaven rules over earth and that Your kingdom is administered by words; words that are spoken to the human heart and carried by Your servants with the same authority with which they left Your lips. I want to be a person whose actions line up with my words. Give me a sensitivity to Your word, however it comes to me, and confirm it in scripture, so that I may be instrumental in bringing heaven's rule to earth. Amen.

Summary:

- There are two coexistent authority structures, seen and unseen, the earthly and heavenly.

- The spiritual realm has pre-eminence over the earthly.

- Authority is administered by words.

- We use the rhema word to go on the offensive against the enemy.

- The rhema word can come without a word being spoken.

- We wear words.

- We need to wear only what God says about us.

- Without obedience to the word of God we have no authority.

- To say one thing and do another means we carry no spiritual authority.

- Righteousness is applying the word received in the heart.

- The servant carries the same authority as the one who sent him.

The Mystic Awakening

Subject Landscape & Chapter Milestones

The Foundation of Authority

7

YOU ARE HERE

The Servant Carries the Authority •
of the one who sent him
No Obedience, No Authority •
We 'wear' words •
Authority administered by words •
Heaven rules over Earth •
Two Authority Structures •

6 P.69 **Authority**

Counter-punch in the opposite spirit •
Going 'out' & coming 'in' •
Tongues •
Gird up the loins •
Need spiritual weapons to defeat spiritual foe •
Wait before battle •
Strong & Courageous •
(Faith & Determination)
(Luke 10:41-42) Martha & Mary •
- One thing needed
- Eternal desposits not taken away
- 'Good' - Benefiting others

5 P.55 **The Making of a Warrior**

Perfect Love: Relationship in His presence •
Overcoming fear •
'One Man' •
Fear: Divided Man •
Gideon: A man divided •
Meditation •
Truth (two layers) aligned •
Romans 10:9-10) 'Saved': Sozo requires: •
- Heart & Mouth

4 P.41 **Man. Utd.**

N
W   E
S

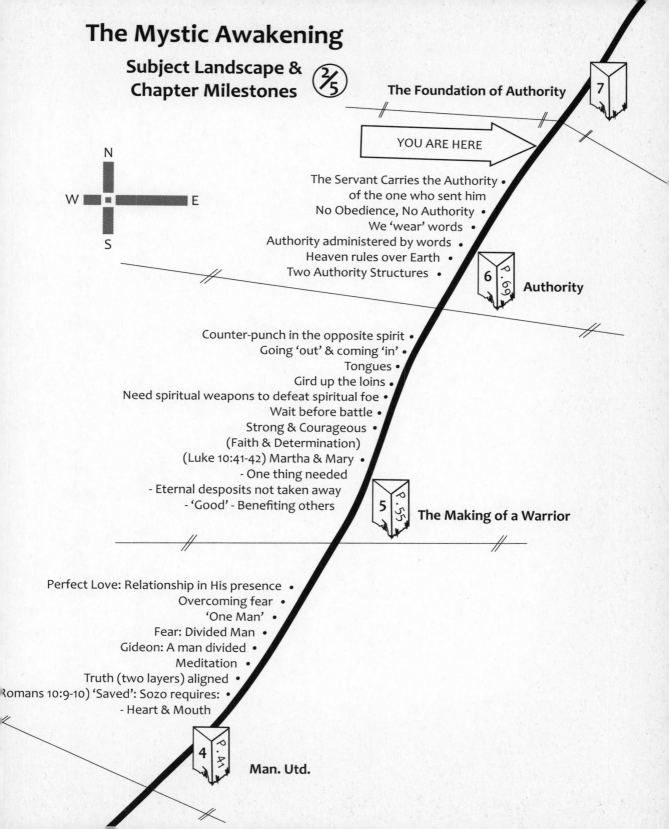

Chapter 7

The Foundation of Authority

'So much more could be achieved
if nobody cared who got the credit!'
President Truman

While there are many similarities between the two coexistent kingdoms of heaven and earth, there are also diametric differences. Jesus explained that leadership in the world is gained by overpowering and exercising dominion over others, whereas leadership in the kingdom of God is marked by humility and service to others. He said,

> *'You know that the rulers of the Gentiles lord it over them, and those who are great exercise over them. Yet it shall not be so among you; but whoever desires to become great among you, let him be your servant. And whoever desires to be first among you, let him be your slave.'*

> Matthew 20:25-27

In saying this, Jesus was not advocating that leadership in the church should be running around serving everyone that they shepherd. We neither see Jesus nor the early church doing this. In the early church when the workload increased because of an increase of numbers, the apostles did not drop everything and serve tables, they delegated others to do that work (1). Jesus likewise did not try and do everything for everyone, instead He poured Himself into 12 men and prepared them to do greater works than He Himself had done.

What is meant in this comparison of kingdoms is best illustrated from a couple of episodes in Israel's history. Firstly, the opening verse of the Book of Joshua says,

> *'After the death of Moses the <u>servant</u> of the LORD, it came to pass that the LORD spoke to Joshua the son of Nun, Moses' <u>assistant</u>, saying.'*

> Joshua 1:1 (Emphasis added)

It is significant and provocative that in this verse the word describing Moses as a *'servant'* (Hebrew: Ebed) describes a lower-ranking servant than the title of *'assistant'* used to describe Joshua, (Hebrew: Sarat). The greatest prophet Israel had known to this point of time had a more lowly title than his understudy! This means that Moses, as a true father, was not insecurely promoting himself, nor lording it over others thinking he was the only anointed of God, but had fully yielded his will to

---

(1) Acts 6:1-6.

the will of the one he was serving (God) and, as a consequence, was pouring himself into his understudy, Joshua. It is important to note that Joshua was no self-appointed intern. He had been handpicked by God (1), and had also proven himself as a man of faith (2), hungry for the presence of God (3) and fully given over to the purposes of God (4).

The same dynamic that existed between Moses and Joshua is repeated in the relationship between Elijah and Elisha. The day in which Elijah transcends earth and is caught up into heaven is rich with insight into the relationship between the two men. The journey they take through various locations is a depiction of the training of Elisha which we will discuss later (5). However, of interest to us here is the first verse of that narrative,

> *'And it came to pass, when the LORD was about to take up Elijah into heaven by a whirlwind, that Elijah went with Elisha from Gilgal.'*

> 2 Kings 2:1

Do you notice anything unusual here? It says that Elijah went with Elisha from Gilgal. Yet, Elisha is the understudy. Surely, Elisha went with Elijah which is what we see as the story unfolds? In having the mantle of Elijah thrown over him, Elisha was marked to be Elijah's replacement and from that day he served him with greater honor than a son who would inherit the family business (6). At one level, the Holy Spirit is drawing our attention to the fact that Elijah was in Elisha as they made that journey. On another level, we are witnessing the humility and servanthood of Elijah. This is the same man who called down fire to kill repeated detachments of soldiers (7) and who killed 450 prophets of Baal in one day (8). What we need to appreciate is that when God told Elijah to anoint Elisha, he also was called to anoint Jehu king of Israel and Hazael king over

---

(1) Numbers 27:18-23; Deuteronomy 3:28. (2) Numbers 14: 6-9. (3) Exodus 33:11. (4) Numbers 32:12. (5) 2 Kings 2:1-14. (6) 2 Kings 2:12; 3:11. (7) 2 Kings 1:10,12. (8) 1 Kings 18: 22, 40.

Syria (1). Here's the amazing thing, he didn't anoint Hazael and Jehu at that time, but more than ten years later, Elisha does! Not only does this confirm that delegated authority carries the same weight as when it left the mouth of God, regardless of time, it also declares that Elijah was in Elisha from the day he was called. So that when God commissioned Elijah to anoint these two kings, he did so, through his protege. Elijah, like Moses before him, had surrendered his will to the will of God in fathering Elisha.

These two great men, Moses and Elijah (who are representative of the Law and the Prophets), in being poured out to God became as servants, mystically duplicating themselves in their understudies so that they would do greater things. In comparing the leadership of the two kingdoms Jesus is asking the same of us, for this is what He Himself has modelled for us. When He later summarises the Old Testament - the Law and the Prophets - by calling us to, *'love your neighbour as yourself'* (2) - He is not only drawing from its content, but also from the spiritual example of those who are considered its pillars.

Meekness Before God
The Means of Authority on Earth

Moses and Elijah both wielded great authority. Moses parted the Red Sea (3) and Elijah called down fire from heaven. The key to their authority is meekness before God. In other words, authority on earth is derived from humility before God (a). It is no coincidence that Moses was called the meekest man on earth Numbers 12:3 explains how he spoke to God face to face (literally: mouth to mouth).

Jesus carried recognizable authority as a pure channel because of His obedience, but the foundation of His authority was His time with God. Like Samuel before Him, none of His

(a) God uses the wilderness to teach this principle. Deuteronomy 8:3.

(1) 1 Kings 19:15-16. (2) Matthew 22:39-40. (3) Exodus 14:21.

words fell to the ground (1), because they weren't derived from a human source. They were Spirit and Life (2) and they had an eternal author. The real reason anyone carries is because they carry God's word. When it comes to public speaking the world emphasises, 'Its all in the delivery'. There is truth to the adage that, 'How you say something, is as important as what you say', however, as I mentioned earlier, the most mundane speakers can, on occasion, bring the most impacting words, purely because God spoke through them (b). The Holy Spirit has chosen to echo this point in the New Testament where it is recorded that Peter and John had great boldness before the religious leaders, though they were ignorant and unlearned men, because, as the scripture recounts, *'they had been with Jesus'* (3).

On one occasion Jesus used a parable to teach the need to be watchful (c) in relation to His return (4). When Peter asked Him whether the parable was applicable only for that generation, Jesus responded by saying,

> *'And the Lord said, Who then is that faithful and wise steward, whom his lord shall make ruler over his household, to give them their portion of meat in due season?*
>
> *Blessed is that servant, whom his lord when he comes shall find so doing. Of a truth I say unto you, that he will make him ruler over all that he has.'*

Luke 12:42-44 (KJV Modernized)

By focusing on His return, Jesus revealed that He was speaking to all the ensuing generations who await His coming. It is not surprising that He also used the occasion to address the nature of leadership. Real leadership, He disclosed, will be carried by those *'so doing'*, which in context means, expectantly waiting in His presence to receive His word. Scripture teaches

(b) God uses unbelievers:

Nebuchadnezzar was humbled because he didn't realize who put him over Babylon (Daniel 4:30-31).

Cyrus was used by God to rebuild Jerusalem (Isaiah 45:1; 44:28).

Caiphas prophesied as high priest (John 11:51).

(c) Watchers are waiters Luke (12:36-37).

---

(1) 1 Samuel 3:19. (2) John 6:63. (3) Acts 4:13. (4) Luke 12:35-48.

that meekness in heaven is the source of authority on earth, and that applies for every age.

In the same vein, the Apostle Paul became the vessel of God to carry His word to the Gentiles changing his name from Saul ('asked for', or 'demanded') to Paul ('little', 'small' or 'humble') (1). Significantly, this name reversal also marked a change in leadership, when Barnabas and Saul suddenly becomes Paul and Barnabas (2).

The Kingdom a Mystery

Whenever Jesus taught about the kingdom He did so using mystical language, so that only those with a heart after God would understand (3). The Bible records that,

> *'All these things Jesus spoke to the multitude in parables; and <u>without a parable He did not speak to them</u>. That it might be fulfilled which was spoken by the prophet, saying, "I will open My mouth in parables; I will utter things kept secret from the foundation of the world."'*
>
> Matthew 13:34-35 (Emphasis added)

In keeping with the mystical nature of discipleship, the Book of Acts records that Jesus was with the Apostles for forty days, *'speaking of the things of the kingdom of God'* (4) and yet does not record what He taught them! It comes as no surprise that in delivering, 'The Sermon on the Mount', (considered 'the Magna Carta' of the kingdom) Jesus once again teaches using veiled speech. This is particularly evident in 'The Beatitudes' (5) which can be regarded as progressive foundations of the kingdom. To understand what He is alluding to at each point requires the spiritual disciple to connect with related passages of scripture (6).

For example, consider, *'Blessed are the meek: for they shall*

(1) Acts 13:9. (2) Acts 13:2,9,13. (3) Matthew 13:10-15. (4) Acts 1:3.
(5) Matthew 5:3-10. (6) 1 Corinthians 2:13-14.

inherit the earth' (1): by flagging key words and recognizing that every scripture has a mate (2), we are drawn to Psalm 37, where we not only find the phrase, *'The meek shall inherit the earth'* (3), but also the repeated promise, *'...shall inherit the earth'*, viz.,

> *'For evildoers shall be cut off; but those who wait upon the Lord, they <u>shall inherit the earth</u>.'*
>
> Psalm 37:9 (Emphasis added)

> *'But the meek <u>shall inherit the earth</u>, and shall delight themselves in the abundance of peace.'*
>
> Psalm 37:11 (Emphasis added)

> *'For those blessed by Him <u>shall inherit the earth</u>, but those cursed by Him shall be cut off.'*
>
> Psalm 37:22 (Emphasis added)

> *'The righteous <u>shall inherit the land</u> (earth)(d), and dwell in it forever.'*
>
> Psalm 37:29 (Emphasis added)

> *'Wait on the Lord, and keep his way, and he <u>shall</u> exalt thee to <u>inherit the land</u> (earth): when the wicked are cut off, you shalt see it.'*
>
> Psalm 37:34 (KJV, Emphasis added)

(d) Hebrew: (H776) 'eres: A noun used interchangeably for either earth or land. It is used almost 2,500 times in the Old Testament (cf. note h chapter 4).

(e) This is not to deny Israel's claim to the physical land promised by God.

Before we consider the characteristics of those who inherit the earth, let's remind ourselves what it is we are to inherit. On one level the earth is us, as earthen vessels (d), and on another, the land is reference to 'The Promised Land', which equates to being, the Land of God's promises or heaven's provision (e).

(1) Matthew 5:5. (2) Isaiah 34:16. (3) Psalm 37:11.

God's Suddenlies

Each of God's 'suddenlies' are preceded by one or more people waiting on Him.

Acts 2:2
preceded by Acts 1:14.

Luke 2:13
preceded by Luke 2:25, 36-38.

Acts 16:26
preceded by Acts 16:25.

cf. Mark 13:36.

Putting the two together, the Promised Land is God manifesting provision of heaven through us. Who are those who 'enter' or inherit these promises? Jesus gives them the title, '*the meek*', and who are they? According to Psalm 37, they are those who '*wait*', are '*blessed*', are '*righteous*' and '*wait*'. Their chief characteristic is waiting. When we find out that the word, '*blessed*' (Hebrew: Barak) carries with it a picture of, 'bending of the knee' to receive a blessing from a superior we have a, 'wild honey' (f) definition of meekness. Meekness, is displayed in waiting on God, humbly bending the knee and being obedient to what God says (righteousness). It's not hard to join the dots: if meekness is the foundation of authority and the meek inherit the promises of God, then obviously what God says to them in the secret place of His presence is the basis for an authority that sees the promise manifest.

Heirs Inherit

Just as someone who marries into a royal line has to learn how to act and carry themselves in society before they exercise their newfound position, so we as believers have to acquire knowledge of our 'higher' lifestyle to access the kingdom. Our key verse is again, '*Blessed are the meek for they shall inherit the earth*' (1). The word, '*inherit*' in both the New and Old Testaments means to be an heir. Simply put, heirs inherit. Because we have been engrafted into the royal line of God's family we have become heirs, but to claim our inheritance we have to grow 'up'. Which, in the context of our discussion, means that we have to learn how to live in His presence. In addressing this need, the Apostle Paul writes to the Galatian church, stating,

(f) Wild honey: John the Baptist was said to have been fed on locusts and wild honey (Matthew 3:4; Mark 1:6).

The Old Testament is referenced as the Law and the Prophets (Matthew 5:17; 7:12), the prophets as instruments of judgment parallel locusts and honey is an idiom of the word (Psalm 19:10; 119:103). 'Wild' honey therefore refers to that untainted by man, i.e. revelation. Therefore, as well as literally eating locusts and honey, there is a hidden message that John the Baptist also was spiritually fed on the prophets and revelation.

(1) Matthew 5:5.

'Now I say, That the heir, as long as he is a child, differs not from a servant, though he be lord of all.'

Galatians 4:1 (KJV Modernized)

As long as we remain '*a child*', we are not yet ready to move into our inheritance. What then, constitutes being a child? Paul, in the same passage goes on to explain,

'Even so we, when we were children, were in bondage under the elements of the world.'

Galatians 4:3

(g) See sidenote (f) chapter 13.

So a child is a person living according to the dictates of this world, evidenced by living a double life by professing one thing and doing another. Our understanding is further refined by the Apostle John, who outlines the elements of the world as, '*the lust of the flesh, the lust of the eyes and the pride of life*' (g) (1). How then does a believer move to maturity and overcome the world? The answer is rooted in meekness because, 'Hope', displayed by expectantly waiting in God's presence, overcomes the lust of the eyes (2), and exercising 'Faith' in God's rhema word defeats issues of the flesh and the limitations of this physical realm (3). However, those who step through the veil into eternity, like Moses and Elijah, move beyond faith to step into knowing Christ experientially (4). This is when they overcome self-glory, otherwise known as pride, by displaying a 'Love' that lays down its life in deference to others. These are marks of a real father (5). Like them, when we step through the world's wilderness of temptation (6), '*in Christ*', we are also given access to the Father's table of provision in heaven (7).

Authority Is Influence

Now that we understand the fundamentals of authority,

(1) 1 John 2:16. (2) cf. Isaiah 40:31 KJ & NIV. (3) Romans 4:19-20 (4) Matthew 7:22-23; Philippians 3:10. (5) 1 Corinthians 4:15. (6) Matthew 4:1-11. (7) Psalm 23:4-5.

what are we to do with this knowledge? Let us consider where everything is heading according to scripture.

Six hundred years before Jesus' birth, Daniel, the prophet, in interpreting a dream for King Nebuchadnezzar, saw the establishment of Christ's kingdom. Nebuchadnezzar had seen a human image in his dream that depicted the major kingdoms who would dominate the known world (1). While there is much debate about the identity and timing of the final kingdom, a kingdom described as consisting of iron and clay, it is clear it is outlived by God's kingdom which would stand forever,

> '*And in the days of these kings shall the God of heaven set up a kingdom which shall never be destroyed; and the kingdom shall not be left to other people; it shall break in pieces and consume all these kingdoms, and it shall stand forever.*'

> Daniel 2:44

According to Nebuchadnezzar's dream, God's kingdom was depicted as being established by a stone cut without human hands, striking the effigy in its feet of iron and clay, and totally destroying it (2). The stone that struck the human monument then became a great mountain and filled the earth (3). On one level, because it is the revealing of heaven, all of this has taken place. However, at an earthly level, part is still to be enacted. The stone is Jesus - the Rock - and in describing it being cut without human hands the imagery declares that this event is clearly God breathed and not in anyway instigated by man. Coming from the mountain is Christ being hurled from heaven to earth (4), while striking the image is a picture of judgment. The first part of this scene has already taken place with Jesus, the word of God, coming to earth, clothed in humanity and dying for the sins of mankind. His vicarious sacrifice at Golgotha was THE judgment of the world and all who avail themselves of

(1) Daniel 2:31-44. (2) Daniel 2:34-35; 45. (3) Daniel 2:35. (4) cf. Hebrews 8:5.

its provision need no longer fear judgment.

That said, what of the stone becoming a great mountain and filling the earth? Jesus declared to Peter that the revelation that He was the Messiah, was, 'the rock' on which Christ would build His church and the powers of hell would not prevail against it (1). So, the church has been growing from its birth, which took place at the cross (h). Until it culminates in subduing all spiritual opposition. I believe the ambiguity that surrounds the emergence of the last kingdom of iron and clay, is deliberate, because it has not yet fully emerged. The church, which is the vehicle for the growth of the kingdom, needs to come to maturity and take on its God-given authority, in preparation to defeat that last kingdom (i).

According to the New Testament writers, Jesus' ascension is His enthronement above all creation, and everything that exists in the earthly and heavenly realms is now placed under His jurisdiction,

> 'And what is the exceeding greatness of his power to us-ward who believe, according to the working of his mighty power, Which he wrought in Christ, when he raised him from the dead, and set him at his own right hand in the heavenly places, Far above all principality, and power, and might, and dominion, and every name that is named, not only in this world, but also in that which is to come.'

Ephesians 1:19-21 (KJV)

> 'Who has gone into heaven, and is at the right hand of God, angels and authorities and powers having being made subject to Him.'

1 Peter 3:22

(h) Jesus is the last Adam (1 Corinthians 15:45). Christ's death corresponds with Adam's deep sleep, where the blood and water from His side (John 19:34) marks the birthing of the church in parallel with Adam's birthing of Eve from his side (Genesis 2:21-22).

(i) An intriguing thought for discussion is that Daniel appears to elaborate his description of the iron and clay, as the mingling of the seed of men with something other than human (Daniel 2:43).

(1) Matthew 16:16-18.

This is acknowledged by Christ Himself when He declared that all authority had been given to Him and then commissioned His followers to go, exercising that authority (1). To the degree that we are seated in heavenly places in Him, is the degree He is in us on earth doing the work. Therefore, between Jesus' ascension and the culmination of all things, the church, the corporate body of believers, is His commissioned servant administrating His delegated authority and doing the work. This is to be a process of ever-expanding influence, till all spiritual opposition (2) is put under His feet,

> *'Then comes the end, when He delivers the kingdom to God the Father, when He puts an end to all rule and all authority and power. For He must reign till he has put all enemies under his feet.'*

1 Corinthians 15:24-25

(1) Matthew 28:18-20. (2) Ephesians 6:12.

Prayer:

Father, all authority is found in You and Your delegated authority is given to those waiting expectantly in Your presence. Like Moses, I long to develop meekness in Your presence so that true fatherhood would be displayed through my life. Give me a heart like Joshua that desires not to depart from Your presence. Give me a heart to practice overcoming all the dictates of this world so that I will manifest a new level of boldness and move into my inheritance here on earth. Amen.

Summary:

- Moses and Elijah served their understudies by pouring themselves into them so they could do greater works.

- Authority on earth is derived from meekness before God.

- Leadership is marked by expectantly waiting in His presence.

- Meekness is displayed in waiting on God, humbly bending the knee and being obedient to what He says.

- Heirs inherit.

- A child lives by the dictates of this world.

- The church, which is the vehicle for the growth of the kingdom, needs to come to maturity and take on its God-given authority, in preparation to defeat the world's final kingdom.

- Between Jesus' ascension and the culmination of all things, the church is the commissioned servant administrating His delegated authority and doing the work.

Chapter 8

God's Love Language

Around a third of the Scripture is poetic. In our modern Bibles that amounts to all the text that is not justified (i.e. ragged-edged text). Poetry stretches far beyond the pages of that which is traditionally recognized as poetic - Job, Psalms, Proverbs, Ecclesiastes and Song of Songs - to include all writings by the prophets, parts of Genesis, Exodus, Numbers, Deuteronomy and more (a). The prophets, Isaiah and Jeremiah, scribe some of the most powerful passages of poetic Scripture as the Spirit of God lifted these mystics into the highest of spiritual experiences. What IS surprising, is that the beauty and form of Hebrew poetry was not openly recognized until

(a) Biblical poetry: the books of Job, Psalms, Proverbs, Song of Songs, Lamentations, Ecclesiastes, Isaiah, Jeremiah, Ezekiel and the minor prophets. Also Genesis 49; Exodus 15; Numbers 23:7-10, 18-24; 24:3-9, 15-24; Deuteronomy 32; Judges 5; 1 Samuel 2; 2 Samuel 22; 2 Samuel 1; Genesis 4:23-24; 1 Kings 8:12-13; Ruth 1:16-17.

When you don't understand what God is saying...

'It is the glory of God to conceal a word...'

'but the glory of kings to search it out.'
Proverbs 25:2

Go back into the glory to understand the download.

the eighteenth century when Bishop Robert Lowth (1710-1787) laid the foundation for a deeper appreciation of it in his work, *Lectures on the Sacred Poetry of the Hebrews*. There were two main reasons such an amount of Scripture lay largely unexplored and unappreciated. Firstly, Western minds were preeminently occupied with searching for religious knowledge, and secondly, they failed to recognize its poetic content because of its lack of adherence to the formal rules of English, Greek and Arabic poetry. It is not so surprising that today we are still prone to miss the voice of the Spirit when it comes in a poetic form outside our western grid.

What fills the heart seems to better express itself through the use of poetry, rather than prose. It is no coincidence that all of the Hebrew mystics caught up in Him, Who is Love, are recorded as using it. Scriptural poetry is full of imagery and metaphor often set to music, making it a heartfelt vehicle to give an alternative view of reality. The Psalms were recited to musical accompaniment as were other poems (1). This visual and auditory (sound) medium indelibly envisions the kingdom metaphorically and in doing so presents not merely elevated language, but elevated vision.

Why is this important? Some of the foundational forms of Hebrew poetry empower us to understand the language of a kingdom that is the expression of God's love and related symbolically by the Spirit of God.

Metaphor

Metaphor is thought of as the essence of poetry. A metaphor is a visual or sensory parallel that provides another view of a situation, thus deepening understanding. For example, the relationship between God and Israel is pictured as a husband and wife (2) and King David's adultery with Bathsheba was

(1) cf. Exodus 15:20-21. (2) Isaiah 54:5.

depicted as a rich man stealing a poor man's one ewe lamb (1). Jesus Himself clothed His speech in a variety of metaphors - seed, trees, landowners, talents - to relate kingdom truths. A very common spiritual metaphor for a person is a tree (2). Animals as well as inanimate objects may also be representations of people, nations, businesses, churches, attitudes or spirits (3). Visions and dreams make heavy use of metaphors, e.g. Peter, who saw the sheet lowered full of unclean animals and was told to, '*kill and eat*' as a message from God to embrace the Gentiles as fellow believers (4). The understanding that what is seen is mostly metaphoric is vital to not being hijacked by emotion when loved ones or graphic images are depicted in a dream or vision.

Personification

Personification is another tool repeatedly used to convey spiritual perspective. Personification is simply when a person is used to represent an issue, church, business or any other subject (5). The classic example in Scripture is where 'wisdom' in the Book of Proverbs is personified as a woman (6). A commonly misunderstood spiritual message is when the visionary's children are seen in a vision or dream. On many occasions this is a depiction of the dreamer's future. In these situations, as is the case when defining any word's use within Scripture, context determines how to interpret the elements, including people, in these scenes. The use of personification means that caution should be applied when a known person features in a dream or vision, do not assume the message is about that person.

Idioms and Word Plays

While not strictly recognized as poetry, idioms provide yet another tool for the Spirit of God to bring a different

---

(1) 2 Samuel 12:3. (2) Psalm 1:3; 92:12-14; Jeremiah 17:8; Proverbs 11:28, 30. (3) Proverbs 14:4; Daniel 7:6; Isaiah 40:4; Zechariah 9:9; Matthew 7:6; 15:26-27. (4) Acts 10:10-17; 11:5-17. (5) Isaiah 23:12; 37:22; 47:1; 54:4. (6) Proverbs 1:20-33; Proverbs chpt. 8-9.

Fallen face: sad (Genesis 4:6).

Closed hand: selfish (Deuteronomy 15:7).

Covered his feet: defecate (1 Samuel 24:7).

Stiffened his neck: became stubborn (2 Chronicles 36:13).

Throat an open grave: speak deceitfully (Psalm 5:9).

Heart and kidneys: thoughts and emotions (Psalm 7:9).

Good eye: generous (Proverbs 22:9).

Evil eye: stingy (Proverbs 23:6).

Lamp go out: die (Proverbs 24:6).

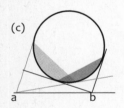

(c)

a   b

Parallelism at times provides two views of a subject from different angles.

(d) Honey: as revelation. (cf. note f chapter 7).

perspective to a kingdom situation. An idiom is an expression that is not automatically understood from its constitutional elements, such as, 'hung out to dry', 'thrown in the deep end', 'foot in mouth' or 'back on track' (b). Similar in some respects are, 'wordplays'. A wordplay is a message in a word or name, like, 'tell-a-vision', 'stone-walling', 'Wal(l)-mart', 'Law-son', 'Connect-i-cut' and 'See-more'.

Parallelism

By far the most commonly used Hebrew poetic device is called 'Parallelism'. This is used where there is a pairing of lines of scripture which run parallel with each other, providing different angles of sight on a subject. The first line presents a picture and the second line amplifies, contrasts or echoes the first and thereby broadens the view. On those occasions what God says may seem obscure, but another look at it from a different angle can help bring clarity (c). For example,

> *'Out of the eater came something to eat*
> *And out of the strong came something sweet.'*

Judges 14:14

In this example, Samson presented a riddle to the Philistines, which depicted eating honey from a lion's carcass (d).

Kingdom truths are similarly communicated to us encoded as personal parables that require knowledge of the author, God, to unlock them (1). The subject of 'Wisdom' has many levels of meaning. The Book of Revelation explains that on one level 'wisdom' is understanding God's use of symbols and metaphors,

> *'Here is the mind that has wisdom:*

(1) cf. Matthew 13:10-11.

The seven heads are seven mountains on which the woman sits.'

Revelation 17:9

While not wanting to get bogged down in technicalities, parallelism has the ability to broaden and visually enhance spiritual realities. This can be seen when the Psalmist writes,

'Your mercy, O Lord, is in the heavens;
and your faithfulness (truth) reaches to the clouds.'

Psalm 36:5 (cf. Psalm 57:10)

The clouds are pretty high, but the heavens, now, that's far out (1)! While there are several divisions in an exhaustive study of Parallelism, for our purposes it is sufficient that we identify what is called, 'emblematic parallelism', in which metaphors are employed in at least one of the lines running parallel. For example,

'As a father pities his children,
So the Lord pities those who fear Him.'

Psalm 103:13

And,

'The ungodly are not so,
But are like the chaff which the wind drives away.'

Psalm 1:4

This is of interest to us as visionaries receiving dreams and visions from God because they, too, are rich in metaphor and imagery. Just as parallelism provides two takes of the same scene, God may provide two views of the same situation in one dream or vision, often marked by a scene change. He may provide consecutive downloads in one night, or over several

Scene Change

(1) cf. James 2:13.

days, about the same subject, where each may present the same situation, but use different metaphors to create a fresh perspective.

Inclusio and Chiasm

Though not regularly seen in dreams and visions, no discussion on Hebrew poetry would be complete without a brief introduction to the terms, 'inclusio' and 'chiasm'. As pointed out in the first chapter, one of the tenets of the ancient mystics was that the scriptures contain two layers of meaning, the exoteric (public) and the esoteric (hidden). Recognition of the use of 'inclusio' or 'chiasms' in a passage of scripture provides major keys to reveal that which would otherwise remain hidden. Inclusio (also called inclusion, frame, envelope, or ring composition), is where a poem begins and ends with a similar line, as in Psalm 104:1 and 35: *'Bless the Lord, O my soul!'* (1). Inclusio not only provides a strong sense of closure, it may also reveal the subject of a passage, or the mission of a person. Earlier it was explained that John's Gospel reported Jesus started His ministry with the cleansing of the temple (2), later He closed it with the same act in the Synoptic Gospels (3), clearly bookending His mission. Similarly, Peter was initially called with a miracle catch of fish (4) and was reinstated with the same (5), which also marked his calling (6). It is interesting, then, that Paul in writing to the Ephesians, says,

'For we are his workmanship (Greek: Poiema), created in Christ Jesus unto good works, which God prepared beforehand that we should walk in them.'

Ephesians 2:10

In the Greek, the one who does the creating is called the 'poietes', or poet. This says we are God's poem! Therefore,

(1) cf. Psalm 8:1, 9. (2) John 2:13-22. (3) Matthew 21:12, 13 ; Mark 11:15-18 ; Luke 19:45, 46. (4) Luke 5:4-11. (5) John 21:5-19. (6) Acts 2:38-41.

we should not be surprised when He may use a Hebrew poetic form, or construct, when communicating to or through us.

Chiasm, pronounced 'ki' as in kite, and 'asm' as in chasm, refers to an inverted X arrangement of information so that parallel terms are in reverse order around a central point.

On either side of the central point of the X, are terms that correlate with each other. For example,

'Make the <u>heart</u> of this people dull, (A)

And their <u>ears</u> heavy, (B)

And shut their <u>eyes</u>; (C)

Lest they see with their <u>eyes</u>, (C)

And hear with their <u>ears</u>, (B)

And understand with their <u>heart</u>...' (A)

Isaiah 6:10

Now look back at Romans 10:9-10 on page 42 and note the chiasm there.

This pattern can be represented a, b, c, c, b, a. Is it coincidence that Jesus quoted this scripture when explaining why He chose to use parables to teach those bound by the cords of religion (1)? The emphasis here is on the eyes, because it is not what we see outwardly, but rather what we see spiritually that is important. As a consequence of failing to exercise the eyes of our spirit, we are prone to miss hearing His voice and our hearts become dull. Developing our spiritual senses by waiting on Him increases our visionary capacity through dreams and visions and brings us to the point where we recognize His voice with clarity and regularity in everyday encounters.

(1) Matthew 13:15.

Coming off the Page

When communicating these spiritual truths God often seeks to get our attention either by repetition or by presenting something out of the ordinary. For example, I recently read an anecdotal report of an unusual increase of birds, called 'Tuis,' in New Zealand. The Tui is a unique bird for many reasons. 'Tui' is the bird's native name, however, its disused English name is the 'Parson Bird', so named because if its black and white plumage. Further to this, it has two voice boxes with which it is able to produce two 'voices' one audible and the other inaudible. Known to be fiercely territorial, the bird had been sighted with more than twenty birds in one tree. The Tui is a honey eater and being the highest in the pecking order amongst birds with similar diets, it chases off competitors at a food source. This bird is known to fly drunk after feeding on fermenting flax, and its mating ritual is to rise at speed in a vertical climb, before stalling and dropping into a power dive. It would appear God is showcasing an unusual increase of a particular spiritual being (bird), which in the past was associated with religion (parson bird). It is a honey eater (1), carries a two-edged sword (two voice boxes), one of which is on a frequency not heard by the natural ear, gets drunk (2), carries authority, and finds union by vertical climbs (3)! For those who have developed their spiritual senses, it is clear that God is about to bring revival to New Zealand, and not only to New Zealand because that country is part of a greater metaphor of the Body of Christ which is entering a 'new zeal-land' (e).

Chiasms can be found in one verse, a few verses or over several verses (often beyond chapter divisions). Even whole books of the Bible may be chiastic in structure. Solomon provides another example of a simple chiasm in one verse,

> *'...Let me see your <u>face</u>, let me hear your <u>voice</u>;*

(e) For those still struggling to come off the printed page of scripture and hear God's voice, consider Solomon, who unearthed 'wisdom' in writing 3000 proverbs about plants, birds, fish and animals (1 Kings 4:32-33).

(1) Psalm 19:9-10. (2) Acts 2:15. (3) Isaiah 40:31.

For your <u>voice</u> is sweet, and your <u>face</u> is comely.'
Song of Songs 2:14 (Tanakh translation, Emphasis added)

To fully appreciate the structuring of words here the whole verse needs to be considered,

'O my dove, that is in the clefts of the rock,
in the secret [place] of the stairs,
let me see your <u>face</u>, (A)
let me hear your <u>voice</u>; (B)
for your <u>voice</u> is sweet, (B)
and your <u>face</u> is comely.' (A)
Song of Songs 2:14 (Tanakh translation, Emphasis added)

The scene opens with Jesus as our Lover addressing us as a humble dove, a beautiful metaphor of purity, gentleness and fidelity (1). This image is enhanced by the contrasted vulnerability of the dove and the security of the rock. The picture paints us as having ascended to the place of protection in His presence, where, in *'the cleft of the rock'*, in the privacy of the *'secret place'* of *'the stairs'* into eternity, He woos us (2). It is in this place that His longing for our presence and His yearning to hear the honey-like smoothness of our voice is climatically captured by the use of the chiasm.

According to Ralph Chittleborough's book, *'Inspired by God'* (f), which maps chiasms through the entire New Testament, recognizing a chiastic structure in a passage of scripture has several benefits. They help to identify:

1. The central point, turning point, theme, crux of the matter.

2. Correlating points acting as a commentary.

3. Context more clearly.

4. The big picture.

(f) Ralph Chittleborough 'Inspired by God'

Available for PDF download at everrest-ministries.com

(1) cf. Song of Songs 5:2; 6:9. (2) cf. Exodus 33:22; Matthew 6:6.

When Isaac blessed Jacob and Esau in Genesis 27:28 and 39 he used a chiasm. However, the chiastic elements are separated by ten verses. To Jacob, Isaac says,

> *'Therefore may God give you*
> *Of the dew of heaven, (A)*
> *Of the fatness of the earth...' (B)*

Genesis 27:28

To Esau, Isaac says,

> *'Behold your dwelling shall be*
> *Of the fatness of the earth, (B)*
> *And of the dew of heaven from above.' (A)*

Genesis 27:39

In this blessing through the mouth of Isaac, God not only lays emphasis on how each son would live, one from heaven and the other from earth, but also points to a buried truth that Jacob, the spiritual man, would ultimately be master of Esau, the fleshly man (1). The Spirit of God has utilized a chiasm to act as inverted bookend (-> <-) to direct attention to this principle.

The worth and relevance of chiasms in revealing the centerpiece, turning point and bigger picture will be seen in a later chapter when discussing the Menorah.

An Old Favorite

To close this exploration of Hebrew poetry a well-known psalm provides an apt example of a metaphor that is often overlooked and also highlights the importance of the repetition of God's word,

> *'Behold, how good and how pleasant it is for brothers dwell together in unity!*
> *It is like the precious ointment upon the head,*

(1) Genesis 27:37.

*that ran down (yarad) upon the beard, even Aaron's beard:
that went down (yarad) to the skirts of his garments;
As the dew of Hermon, and as the dew that descended (yarad)
upon the mountains of Zion: for there the Lord commanded
-- the blessing, even life forevermore.'*

Psalm 133:1-3 (Tanakh translation)

The phrase, '*how good and pleasant it is that brothers dwell together*', contains a hidden metaphor. The verb, '*dwell together*' (Hebrew: shevet yahad), is a legal term meaning to live in joint tenancy; that is, to hold land in joint ownership without dividing it up among separate parties. The psalm is not primarily about getting along with one another in church, or about harmony in the home, but is about '*brothers*' holding land together. While the Jews believe this speaks about the reunification of Israel and Judah, it is also about Christ cohabiting in us, for the Book of Hebrews tells us that He is not ashamed to call us '*brothers*' (1)! The unity described here climaxes in eternal life.

This eternal life is the result of the high priest's anointing running down onto his bodily garments, this is not only previewed in the earthly ministry of Christ (2), but also in His heavenly ministry, as the Body of Christ is anointed from our Head (3). Once again, the critical factor for the manifestation of heaven on earth is oneness with Him. The psalm continues by describing that union as dew falling from Mount Hermon (g), onto those who stand out for God (the mountains). These are the ones who receive His rhema word of blessing, which has life in itself (4).

(g) Hermon: (H2768) = Lofty, the lofty one.

In this psalm the Hebrew word, 'yarad' occurs three times in succession, twice in reference to the oil, 'running down' upon Aaron's beard and robes and once in reference to the dew of Mount Hermon 'descending' on the spiritual mountains

(1) Hebrews 2:11. (2) Matthew 9:20-21. (3) Ephesians 1:22-23; Acts 2:33; Hebrews 4:14. (4) John 6:63.

of Israel. The repetition occurring three times in this context speaks about the fullness of the Spirit being poured out. In doing so this psalm builds to a climax, which is not realized until Christ is enthroned in heaven, a climax of unity that could not be achieved until we were vessels cleansed and able to accommodate His Spirit.

Application (Coming off the page):

Spend a few minutes each day looking at objects that fill your world. Ask yourself what they would represent as a metaphor in a dream or vision. For example, a chair could be a resting place, a seat of authority, or an invitation to fellowship. A pen could be an invitation to write, may speak of a contract, or it may simply be prompting a letter to be written. A flower may be an expression of love, a person, a preview to fruitfulness, or it may represent the glory of God (Matthew 6:28-29). Do you get the idea? Now look around and what do you see?

Summary:

- A third of scripture is poetry.

- What fills the heart is better expressed through poetry, rather than prose.

- Poetry is not just elevated language, it is elevated vision.

- Metaphors provide a visual and sensory parallel of a situation, which deepens understanding.

- Personification is a poetic device where a person is used to represent an issue, church, or business, etc.

- The use of parallelism provides different lines of sight on a subject.

- A scene change in a dream or vision may indicate the use of parallelism.

- Inclusion is where a poem starts and ends with the same line of verse.

- A chiasm is an X structure, where parallel terms are in reverse order around a central point.

- The use of chaisms help identify:
  - the central point
  - correlating points
  - context
  - the big picture

- The critical factor for the manifestation of heaven on earth is oneness with Him.

Chapter 9

Tongues

*'For he who speaks in a tongue does not speak to men
but to God, for no one understands him;
however, in the spirit he speaks mysteries.'*

1 Corinthians 14:2

Any discussion on mysticism, the revealing of mysteries, would not be complete without consideration for the infilling of the Spirit and the subsequent manifestation of speaking in other tongues. This phenomena, which marked the receipt of power by the early church, and at one time distinguished Pentecostal assemblies from mainstream Christianity, has become a mere token of expression as the Charismatic church has sought acceptance by the world. Speaking in tongues has become unfashionable amongst many who do not want to appear weird to non-believers. It is in danger of being replaced

(b) New creation means a totally new type of being.

New (G2537). καινοσ kainos; fem. kaine, neut. kainon, adj. New. Qualitatively new, <u>not before known</u>, as contrasted with neos (G3501), temporally new.

by a so-called, 'spirit of excellence'. Now there is no problem with doing things well, however, a call to excellence may be nothing more than a response to poor performance and lackluster presentation. When this is the case the church is in danger of falling into the trap of wanting to look good outwardly at the cost of time before Him (looking good inwardly). When presentation is our focus, we are found to be measuring ourselves against the world. The yardstick is wrong. If this is the case, we may be guilty of being conformed instead of transformed.

We are meant to stand out. In a world that has little appreciation beyond what can be rationally explained, believing in an invisible God is indeed weird. Believing He became a man is beyond human comprehension. Believing that He died for our sins is beyond the bounds of what is considered normal and believing that He - Creator of the universe - could have relationship with us as individuals is deemed absurd! Therefore, it is not surprising that speaking what the rational mind considers gibberish, has also fallen out of vogue (a). We need to keep before us that as Christians we are a completely new race of beings (1) (b) and it is normal for people of a different race to speak a different language. On this score, let's join the dots, and acknowledge that within the Western church there has been a loss of power corresponding to its denial of the value of speaking in other tongues.

To the uninitiated the various purposes of speaking in tongues may be lumped together into one category, but the New Testament delineates four expressions of the gift. What

(1) 2 Corinthians 5:17.

may surprise you further is that there is more written about speaking in tongues in the Old Testament than in the New. As others have already covered the subject of tongues from a New Testament standpoint I intend only to briefly outline the four expressions of the gift shown there, and in the process open the connection to their Old Testament foundations.

Four Expressions of the Gift

On the Day of Pentecost (1) the outpouring of the Spirit that took place is an example of tongues as a 'sign'. This is where the Holy Spirit may speak through a person in a recognized language otherwise unknown to the mouthpiece He is using. When my good friend Adam F. Thompson and I were in Seattle in 2010, Adam began speaking in tongues as he was ministering to people. He used an expression, 'Ramah Sukkah', repeatedly. A woman came up to him afterwards and asked whether he knew what the expression meant, to which Adam replied that he did not. Later on that same tour we were ministering, in a Messianic church in Florida, where he again found himself using the same expression when praying for people. A woman asked the same question and then explained that he was using Hebrew and that the literal interpretation was 'Ramah = Height/ High, and Sukkah = Canopy/Booth'. His words, which he did not understand, were, in effect, calling the Tabernacle of heaven to earth for each of those receiving prayer!

In the eighth chapter of the Book of Romans, another use of the gift is explained,

> *'Likewise the Spirit also helps in our weaknesses. For we do not know what we should pray for as we ought, but the Spirit Himself makes intercession for us with groanings which cannot be uttered. Now He who searches the hearts knows what the mind of the Spirit is, because He makes intercession*

(1) Acts 2:1-13.

for the saints according to the will of God.'

Romans 8:26-27

Here the groanings of the Holy Spirit expressed through us are described as intercessory in nature. In context, this passage describes the world as experiencing birth pangs, awaiting for sons of God to emerge, just as a woman who is in labor. Then, in using the bridging word, *'Likewise'*, the Apostle Paul is drawing the parallel that the Spirit similarly uses us to bring His purposes to pass, or perhaps better, birth God's will in a situation.

Next, in explaining the use of the Gifts of the Spirit, in a corporate gathering, to the Corinthian church, Paul explains how tongues and their interpretation combine to constitute prophecy and are to edify the church (1).

Finally, the New Testament records that speaking in tongues builds and edifies the inner spiritual man,

'But you, beloved, building yourselves up on your
most holy faith,
praying in the Holy Spirit.'

Jude 1:20

And so the New Testament openly documents four expressions of the gift of speaking in tongues. Most think that it ends there and that is the limit of the gift. What we need to realize is that these four expressions of the gift are also demonstrated in the Old Testament and that this document goes deeper in unearthing the mysteries of tongues. The New Testament writers were only partially documenting what can be seen through the veiled window of the Old Testament. When the Apostle Paul writes, *'I thank my God, I speak with tongues more than you all,'* (2), he does so because he has a

---

(1) 1 Corinthians 12:7-11; 14:2-5, 13. (2) 1 Corinthians 14:18.

deep appreciation and understanding of the Old Testament due to his being a student of the Law. Brief exploration of this will allow us to see the foundation from which the New Testament gift of speaking in tongues is drawn and give a 'depth of field' to better understand its worth and expression.

Intercession

The record of Romans 8, which describes using intercession to birth the will of God in a given situation is seen in at least a couple of places in the Old Testament.

The first of these is in the life of Hannah as she comes before God expressing her grief over being barren (1). It is no coincidence that Eli, the priest, in observing her pray, thought that she was drunk, when he could not hear her voice and only saw her lips move (2). To better understand the parallel we will overlay a 'lens' in the form of scripture from the writings of Paul. In addressing the Ephesian church he exhorts them, *'not to be drunk with wine...but be filled with the Spirit'* (3). In pouring her heart out before God, Hannah was heard and gave birth to Samuel. Hannah's seemingly drunken prayer before God pictures for us, 'in type', how the Holy Spirit may use tongues to carry an inexpressible burden of heart, that make no sense to the natural mind. This dimension of the gift of speaking in other tongues gives us a vocabulary that human words cannot express. This means that God has given us a vehicle to carry His purposes when we don't really know what or how to pray. And could it also be that when we are faced with issues beyond our comprehension to deal with, that these were always meant to be released to God through praying in the Spirit? If so, then, like Hannah, we would also be able to get up, eat and our countenance would no longer be heavy (4), rather than numbing the pain with drugs and alcohol.

(1) 1 Samuel 1:2-18. (2) 1 Samuel 1:12-13. (3) Ephesians 5:18. (4) 1 Samuel 1:18.

This ability to bring to birth God's purposes through praying in the Spirit is also displayed in 'type' in the life of Elijah. After three years of drought, which would only break at the word of Elijah (1), God instructed Elijah to go to Ahab, the king of Israel, and tell him that it was about to rain (2). Between God's promise of rain and it actually falling to earth, Elijah was pitted in battle against the prophets of Baal. Elijah defeated the false prophets in a challenge to call down fire to consume a burnt offering and in doing so he turned Israel's heart back to God. After having all the representatives of Baal killed, Elijah climbed to the top of Mount Carmel, cast himself to the ground, and *'put his face between his knees'* (3). This position is associated with birthing. Elijah is not merely acting the scene out, he is bringing forth the promise of rain through intercessory prayer. The rain is a metaphor for the blessing of God, being released through praying in the Spirit.

It is interesting that although Elijah had been given God's word promising rain, he still needed to 'birth' it in persistent prayer, to bring it from the heavens to the earth. When his servant sees a cloud the size of a man's hand rising from the sea, he is seeing the promise in Elijah (the hand and heart are the same size) bursting through his master's heart (as a portal), into this world (4). Now, to really nail the fact that Elijah is praying in the Spirit, we need to strip away the camouflage of the challenge to the prophets of Baal to see what is really happening here.

Every victorious battle scene from the Old Testament prefigures elements of Christ's victory over satan at the cross, and this one is no different. The challenge was for the two camps - prophets of Baal and Elijah - to lay a bullock upon an altar and the god who answered by fire would prove Himself God (5). When the advocates of false religion are unable to

---

(1) 1 Kings 17:1. (2) 1 Kings 18:1. (3) 1 Kings 18:42. (4) 1 Kings 18:44.
(5) 1 Kings 18:23-44.

coerce their god to send fire, Elijah restores the altar of the Lord at the time of the evening offering. It is here that we need to document some land marks:

1. Time of the evening offering (3pm) (v29, 36)
2. Restores the altar of the Lord (v30)
3. Uses 12 stones to build the altar (v32)
4. Trench dug holding 2 measures of seed (v32)
5. Wood in order (v33)
6. Cut sacrifice (v33)
7. 4 barrels of water poured on offering (v33)
8. Repeated 3 times (v35)
9. Calls for fire to prove he is God's servant (v36-37)
10. Rain falls after sending his servant 7 times (v44)

Elijah	Reference	Jesus	Reference
Rebuilt the altar	1 Kings 18:30	Jesus' mission	John 2:13 ff/Matthew 21:12 ff
Evening Offering	1 Kings 18:36	3pm	Matthew 27:45
12 Stones	1 Kings 18:31	12 Disciples	John 6:67
Trench holding 2 measures	1 Kings 18:32	Double portion	Colossians 1:15
Wood in order	1 Kings 18:33	Cross	John 19:17
Cut sacrifice	1 Kings 18:33	Messiah cut off	Daniel 9:26
4 Barrels of water	1 Kings 18:33	4 Corners of world	Revelation 7:1
3 Times	1 Kings 18:34	Complete/Full	Daniel 10:2
Servant	1 Kings 18:36	Servant	Isaiah 52:13
Fire	1 Kings 18:38	Judgement	Luke 17:29
Fire	1 Kings 18:38	Consecration	Leviticus 9:24; Acts 2:3
Rain after 7 times	1 Kings 18:44	Holy Spirit falls	Acts 2:1

Table a: Carmel and the Cross

Looking at the table above there is an obvious parallel between Elijah's evening sacrifice and God's offering in Christ. Both were sacrificed at the time of the evening offering. The twelve stones are representative of the hearts of the disciples

117

(c) Stones are elsewhere described as witnesses (Joshua 24:26-27), as a pillow (Genesis 28:11, 18), the cover of a well (Genesis 29:2-3) and that which a sling launches (1 Samuel 17:40, 49). All of these references show that stones may represent human hearts: people witness, hearts rest, our heart is a well and out of the heart, the mouth speaks. So, in using 12 stones, which as noted represent the 12 tribes of Israel (v31), we are also looking at the 12 hearts of the disciples.

(d) Water can be a metaphor for words (Ephesians 4:26), and four symbolism for the four corners of the world (Revelation 7:1), i.e. the judgment of the world laid on Christ.

(e) Three as completeness: Luke 13:21, 32; Acts 9:9; 10:16.

(f) Fire: judgment (Revelation 18:8) and consecration (Numbers 31:22).

(g) Pentecost (Feast of Weeks) is 7x7 days after Passover (Leviticus 23:15-22).

(c). The trench was to hold two measures of seed (1), in keeping with Christ as the Firstborn who received a double blessing (2). The wood put in order prefigures the cross. Elijah like Jesus is as the servant of Jehovah. The four barrels of water represent the world's judgment (d). The dousing with water is done three times to convey its completeness (e). Finally, fire represents judgment and consecration (f). In Christ's offering, God meted out judgment on mankind and also His approval by sending fire from heaven (3).

Now, we can see that, prefiguring the cross, heaven is opened and the Holy Spirit sent, represented by the rain of refreshing (g). Note that in climbing the mountain to take up an intercessory position Elijah prefigures Christ's ascension and intercessory role in sending the Holy Spirit from heaven. In Christ, we are both here and in heaven. His praying beyond the veil is His outpouring into our hearts, manifesting in the mystery of tongues of intercession through our mouths.

Tongues and Interpretation = Prophecy

When Moses asked the Lord what to do should Israel not believe that he had met with Him, God gave instructions on how to perform signs to convince them that their pending deliverance from Egypt was truly a word from God.

The first sign was that Moses was to throw his rod to the ground where it would become a serpent before Israel (4). When you consider that this was the same rod that Moses used to divide the Red Sea (5), you realize that we are seeing a prophetic enactment of Hebrews 4:12. In throwing the rod to the ground we are witnessing Jesus, the word of God (6), coming to earth; and in the rod becoming a snake, we are onlookers of Jesus becoming sin for us (7).

God then gave another sign (8). He told him to put his hand in his garment (bosom: KJV) and then pull it out. In pulling out

(1) 1 Kings 18:32. (2) Colossians 1:15, 18; Deuteronomy 21:17. (3) Acts 2:3. (4) Exodus 4:2-4. (5) Exodus 14:16, 21. (6) John 1:1. (7) Numbers 21:7; 2 Corinthians 5:21. (8) Exodus 4:6-7.

his hand it became leprous. Leprosy in scripture is a picture of sin (h). The act of Moses putting his hand in his garment and then drawing it out is symbolically showing Jesus as the right hand of God (1), taking on humanity's sin. Moses was then to place his now leprous hand again into his garment and this time when he drew it out it was clean. This is a picture of Jesus taking humanity's sin to the center of the earth - or hell (2) - the holding place for sin, depositing it there and then resurrecting, free from sin.

Finally, for those who would not believe the first two signs God instructed Moses to take water from the river and pour it out on the dry ground and the water would become blood (3). Water turning into blood is primarily a sign of two things in scripture. It symbolizes judgment and the subsequent loss of life (4), or it conveys justification at the acceptance of an offering (5). For those who deny Christ's incarnation, death for sin and resurrection, symbolized by the first two signs, there will be judgment even as water turning to blood (i).

You may be wondering what this has to do with tongues and interpretation? The Old Testament examples explained above provide an important sequence of events for us to see the significance of what follows. Subsequent to these events, Moses, angers the Lord, by insisting he is, '*slow of speech*', and has, '*a heavy and awkward tongue*' (6). God's response is to send Moses' brother, Aaron, to accompany him so that Moses can speak to Aaron what God says, and Aaron in turn, can convey the message to the people.

> '*You must speak to him and put the words in his mouth; and I will be with your mouth and <u>with his mouth</u> and will teach you what you shall do. He shall speak for you to the people, acting as a mouthpiece for you, and you shall be as God to him.*'
>
> Exodus 4:15-16 (AMP, Emphasis added)

(h) In relating the parallel between leprosy and sin consider that the offering for the cleansing of a leper is to take two turtledoves, put one in a earth vessel, kill it and dip the other bird in the blood to sprinkle the blood of cleansing (Leviticus 14:4-7). Two birds is a prophetic picture of two heavenly beings, Jesus and the Holy Spirit. The bird placed in the earthen vessel, of course, is Jesus who came to earth and took on humanity (2 Corinthians 4:7) and was killed for our sin. The bird subsequently dipped in the blood is the Holy Spirit, Who now spreads the message of deliverance from sin throughout the earth.

(i) In scripture water to blood can depict:

- Offering: David 2 Samuel 23:15-17.

- Judgment: Exodus 4:9; 7:19, 21.

- Birth: John 19:34.

- Defeat turned to victory: 2 Kings 3:23.

(1) Genesis 48:18; Matthew 22:44; 26:64. (2) Ezekiel 31:16. (3) Exodus 4:9. (4) Exodus 7:19-21. (5) 2 Samuel 23:15-17. (6) Exodus 4:10 AMP.

Now, in context of all that precedes Moses' stuttering and Aaron's reissuing of what he has said, we are witnessing a type of tongues and interpretation. Jesus has died for sin, that the Holy Spirit may be poured out, and one of His expressions is tongues and interpretation. This passage also explains that Aaron is not merely the translator of what God says through Moses, for it states, that God will be *'with his (Aaron's) mouth'*. This is in keeping with the spiritual gifts in that the Holy Spirit is both the giver of the tongue and, in a completely separate endowment, the interpreter as well. Moses, in type, is speaking a mystery, which in turn needs a gift of interpretation so that when combined, God's word of prophecy is brought forth (j).

(j) Tongues and interpretation constitute prophecy (1 Corinthians 14:5).

Personal Edification

When the prophet Samuel anointed Saul to be King of Israel he gave several words of knowledge to confirm this (1). Like the earlier material in this chapter, each of the encounters prophesied by Samuel has deeper spiritual significance than its face value. For the sake of brevity I will discuss only the last one.

> *'After that you shall come to the hill of God where the Philistine garrison is. And it will happen, when you have come there to the city, that you will meet a group of prophets coming down from the high place with a stringed instrument, a tambourine, a flute, and a harp before them; and they will be <u>prophesying</u>. Then the Spirit of the Lord will come upon you, and you will <u>prophesy</u> with them and be <u>turned into another man</u>.'*

1 Samuel 10:5-6 (Emphasis added)

The company of prophets is described as playing musical instruments and prophesying. The word for *'prophesying'* in

(1) 1 Samuel 10:1-7.

Hebrew describes someone caught up in ecstatic utterance. The root of the word is, 'Naba/Nabi', which means, 'to bubble up, to boil forth, to pour forth words'. With this insight it is easy to see that here is yet another example of speaking in tongues from the Old Testament (1). The passage continues to say that when Saul meets the prophets that the Spirit of God will come upon him, and he likewise, will prophesy and be *'turned into another man'*, as a consequence. That other man is Christ, or Saul's spiritual man. Saul, in speaking ecstatically, is 'in type' effectively 'building himself up' by praying in the Spirit (2). One final thought on this scenario is that the prophets who were playing music and speaking ecstatically, were stepping into the prophecy that went before them from their own mouths (k). Therefore, another powerful benefit of praying in tongues is to release ones' destiny.

(k) We step into the words that go before us from our own mouths.

Another overlooked Old Testament reference to tongues being used to edify is found in the Psalms.

'Out of the mouths of babes and unweaned infants You have established strength because of Your foes, that You might silence the enemy and the avenger.'

Psalm 8:2 (Literal translation)

The incoherent sounds that babies make may be compared to the sounds that emanate from our mouths as we pray in tongues. This passage declares that such is a vehicle for *'establishing strength'*. The word, *'establish'* used here means, 'to lay the foundation of a building'. We are that building. Once again, encoded within the script of the Law, is yet another example of speaking in tongues (l). Tongues, not only build us up, but as this passage shows, it also gives the enemy no words of doubt and unbelief with which to condemn us (3)!

(l) cf. Matthew 21:16.

(1) cf. John 7:37-38. (2) Jude 1:20; cf. 1 Corinthians 14:4. (3) Ephesians 4:27; 1 Peter 5:8.

Tongues as a Sign

At the Tower of Babel, mankind were all of *'one lip and one speech'* (1), literally meaning that they all spoke the same language, but as the lip can be also considered the source of our words, this statement may also be understood to say they were of one heart and mind. In defiance of God's command to Noah to go forth and populate the earth (2), men rebelliously converged in the Plain of Shinar, and attempted to make themselves the center of worship by their achievements in erecting a tower into heaven (3). In response, God gave them different tongues (languages), so that they were forced to diverge from both that place and their plan. In forcing mankind to scatter from one another, God's judgment was a sign of the disunity that existed between God and man.

Seven hundred years before the birth of Christ, God hinted that a new level of convergence awaited Israel, when He said through the prophet Isaiah,

> *'For with stammering lips and another tongue will he speak to this people. To whom he said, This is the rest wherewith you may cause the weary to rest; and this is the refreshing: yet they would not hear.'*

Isaiah 28:11-12 (KJV Modernized)

On one level this spoke of Israel going into captivity in Babylon and, later, returning to Israel to be freed from their idolatry. However, this verse also speaks on another level of deeper things. The Apostle Paul quotes it in addressing the Corinthian church (4) and Paul uses it to argue that tongues are a sign to unbelievers (5).

With this background, the Day of Pentecost takes on new meaning, as unbelieving pilgrims witness the disciples using

(1) Genesis 11:1. (2) Genesis 8:16-17. (3) Genesis 11:1-4. (4) 1 Corinthians 14:21. (5) 1 Corinthians 14:22.

foreign and previously unlearned languages to declare the wonderful works of God (1). The phenomenon that took place caught people's attention because, together with Peter's sermon, it was responsible for 3000 souls entering the kingdom (2). However, it is the incident back in Genesis, at the Tower of Babel, that shows its true significance. Both accounts record people speaking different languages and in both accounts the people were of one mind and heart (3), yet there is a diametric difference in their unity. The first group were building an edifice to glorify man (m), the second were in the Spirit building the Body of Christ, to glorify God. True unity is not a facet of any outward observance: color, dress or even language, but is rather a faculty of the Spirit (4). This means that it is not the language that issues from our mouths that is important, but the heart from which it emanates.

(m) Bricks vs Stone: (Genesis 11:3-4; Daniel 2:34-35.

Man-made vs. Natural

Glory of man vs. Glory of God.

What is truly exciting about identifying the Old Testament roots to the New Testament gift of speaking in tongues is that in unearthing origins we also discover elements of the gift that are not yet fully unpacked due to our shallow understanding of the New Testament. In the Genesis account of what has been identified as, 'tongues for a sign', God presents a seedbed of opportunity to seize what is ours, when He says,

> 'And the Lord said, Behold, the people is one, and they have all one language; and this they begin to do: and now nothing will be *restrained* from them, which they have *imagined* to do.'

> Genesis 11:6 (KJV, Emphasis added)

The underlined words in this passage have some rather interesting roots. The word translated, '*restrained*' is the Hebrew '*Basar*' which means 'to harvest', and the word, '*imagined*'

(1) Acts 2:1-11. (2) Acts 2:41. (3) Genesis 11:1; Acts 2:1. (4) 1 Corinthians 6:17.

'Zamam', derives its meaning from the idea of talking to oneself in a low voice, as if arriving at some conclusion. It denotes the action of fixing thought on an object so as to acquire it. This is simply too coincidental to be coincidence. Do you mean that when we purposely murmur in tongues focusing on building for His glory - and nothing is impossible - the 'seed' that leaves our mouth is guaranteed a harvest?! Yes, that's exactly what I mean!

Prayer:

Now pray in tongues for 30 minutes, realizing that:

- like Hannah, this is your opportunity to pour out your heart before God that which is otherwise inexpressible to men.

- like Elijah, you are bringing to birth the promises God has placed in your heart.

- like Moses, God is bringing heaven to earth through you.

- like the promise to Saul, you are being changed into 'another man'.

- like the prophets who met Saul, your destiny is being unfurled before you.

- as a building, you are laying your own foundation.

- with focus on building for His glory, you are releasing 'seed' that does the impossible!

Summary:

- Tongues marked the receipt of power by the early church.

- Speaking in tongues is in danger of being subtly replaced by a 'spirit of excellence'.

- Christians are a completely new race of beings.

- There are four expressions of speaking in tongues outlined in the New Testament:
  - tongues for a sign
  - tongues for intercession
  - tongues for interpretation
  - tongues for personal edification.

- Each of these has Old Testament roots.

- The story of Hannah was the OT foundation of tongues for intercession.

- Tongues give us a vocabulary that understandable words cannot express.

- We are given the ability to birth the promises and purposes of God through praying in the Spirit.

- Elijah's battle with the prophets of Baal on Mount Carmel prefigures Christ's death upon the cross and the subsequent outpouring of heaven's rain.

- Tongues and interpretation was prefigured in the Old Testament when Moses, the stutterer, and Aaron, the prophet, combine to be God's mouthpiece.

- When King Saul joined the prophets by speaking ecstatically he demonstrates tongues for personal edification as he was meant to be changed into another man.

- The Tower of Babel was a precursor of 'tongues as a sign'.

- When focusing on building for His glory, tongues releases seed that is guaranteed a harvest.

The Mystic Awakening

Subject Landscape & Chapter Milestones

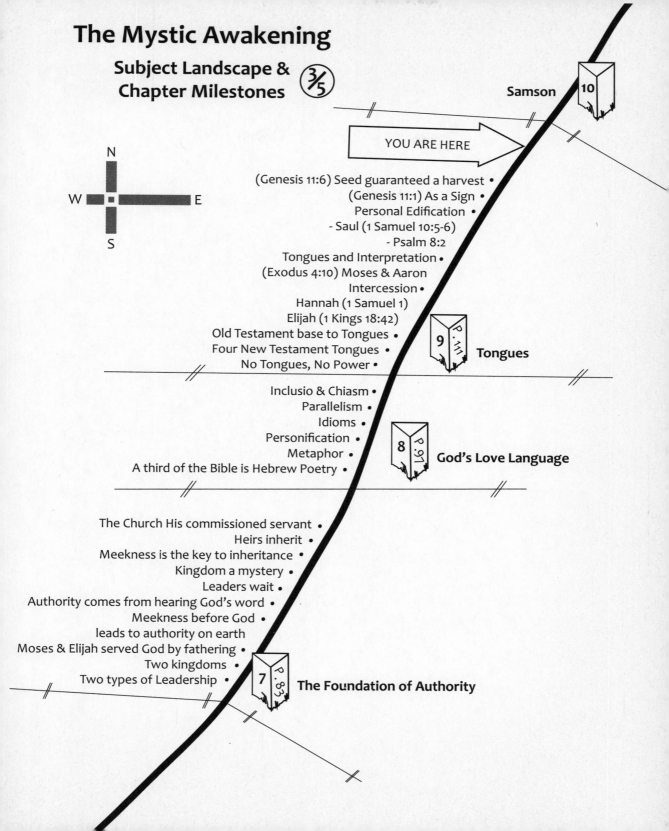

Samson

10

YOU ARE HERE

(Genesis 11:6) Seed guaranteed a harvest •
(Genesis 11:1) As a Sign •
Personal Edification •
- Saul (1 Samuel 10:5-6)
- Psalm 8:2
Tongues and Interpretation •
(Exodus 4:10) Moses & Aaron
Intercession •
Hannah (1 Samuel 1)
Elijah (1 Kings 18:42)
Old Testament base to Tongues •
Four New Testament Tongues •
No Tongues, No Power •

9 P.111   **Tongues**

Inclusio & Chiasm •
Parallelism •
Idioms •
Personification •
Metaphor •
A third of the Bible is Hebrew Poetry •

8 P.91   **God's Love Language**

The Church His commissioned servant •
Heirs inherit •
Meekness is the key to inheritance •
Kingdom a mystery •
Leaders wait •
Authority comes from hearing God's word •
Meekness before God •
leads to authority on earth
Moses & Elijah served God by fathering •
Two kingdoms •
Two types of Leadership •

7 P.83   **The Foundation of Authority**

N
W   E
S

Chapter 10

Samson

The Unsung Hero

The previous chapter reveals the importance of the narratives of the Old Testament in equipping us to harness the kingdom that the New Testament declares is ours through Christ. In fact, as we will see in this chapter, without the insights provided by the Old Testament we are incapable of truly comprehending the kingdom to which we have been called. That said, it is with much anticipation that we now take a fresh look at the life and ministry of Samson. Through mystic eyes, we can uncover more than was previously associated with his ministry, not the least of which is further understanding of the Baptism of the Spirit and speaking in tongues.

If it weren't for the mention of him in the faith chapter of the Book of Hebrews (1) most would come away from reading

(1) Hebrews 11:32.

129

the record of Samson's life with a sense of despair of a life which failed to reach its potential. Indeed, some have dared to label him, 'The weak strong man'. However, it is possible that such assessments fall way short of the truth. The incredible alignment of his life with that of Christ may suggest a greater leading by the Spirit of God, than had previously been attributed to him. If so, he is a true hero of the faith.

Finding Our Bearings

Just as when you fly over your own city you notice significant landmarks that have become familiar to you at ground level, so it is in reading through Samson's narrative that bastions of the Gospel leap above the landscape to pinpoint your location. So let's dig right in by considering that Samson was betrayed by his own countrymen when leaders from the tribe of Judah came and bound him to take him to the Philistines (1). When you realize that Judah is a possible Old Testament parallel to Judas in the New, you go, 'Aha' (2). Our attention is further aroused, when subsequently, after killing a thousand Philistines, Samson essentially cries out, '*I thirst!*' (3), in accordance with the words of Christ upon the cross (4). After which he rather coincidentally experiences a 'resurrection' (5). At this point it is evident that another script is being played out here. A deeper and broader excavation is required.

Killing 1000 Philistines

When thinking about Samson, the most common association people have is the betrayal by Delilah. However, the epicenter of the story of Samson is the episode where he killed a thousand Philistines with a jawbone of an ass. What does a jawbone speak of symbolically? It speaks of the mouth or, more specifically, the words that emanate from it. And

(1) Judges 15:11-14. (2) Matthew 27:1-2. (3) Judges 15:18. (4) John 19:28. (5) Judges 15:19.

what does an ass represent? Within scripture it is a depiction of a faithful servant (a). The jawbone of an ass is then, 'the words of a servant' or the 'Servant Word'. Further understanding is provided by the prophet Isaiah, when he says,

> *'A little one shall become <u>a thousand</u>,*
> *And a small one a strong <u>nation</u>....'*

Isaiah 60:22

Here we discover that a thousand is as a nation (b). Therefore, Samson is representatively defeating a nation of Philistines. When we discover that the root of the name, 'Philistine' is, 'Migrant, Traveller, Wanderer' and make the appropriate association with satan, who is depicted as wandering '*to and fro throughout the earth*' (1), we see that Samson is, in type, defeating a nation of evil spirits with the words of a servant. This is reiterated when Samson, in speaking to God, declares, '*You have given this great deliverance by the hand of Your servant...*' (2), which is also, of course, a reference to a more readily recognized Suffering Servant (3). The record of Samson killing a thousand Philistines is actually a prophetic enactment of Christ's victory at the cross!

A Visit to Gaza

In the record of Samson's life it is recorded twice that he, '*judged Israel twenty years*' (4). Why is it mentioned twice? Each of these statements appear to be a eulogy marking the death of Samson, and with good reason. Immediately after the first apparent death of Samson the Holy Spirit provides unseen footage of what took place, for Christ, beyond the veil of death,

> '*Now Samson went to Gaza and saw a harlot there, and went in to her. When the Gazites were told, "Samson has come*

(a) Ass in scripture as a servant. Zechariah 9:9; Matthew 21:5 & Matthew 11:29; Luke 22:27.

(b) Hebrew 1000 also means clan

(H505) elep: A masculine noun meaning a thousand or clan.

(Genesis 20:16; Judges 6:15).

(1) Job 1:7; 2:2. (2) Judges 15:18. (3) Isaiah 52:13-53:12. (4) Judges 15:20; 16:31.

here!" They surrounded the place and lay in wait for him <u>*all night*</u> *at the gate of the city. They were quiet* <u>*all night*</u>*, saying, "In the morning, when it is daylight, we will kill him."*

And Samson lay low till midnight; then <u>*he arose at midnight*</u>*, took hold of the doors of the gate of the city and the two gateposts, pulled them up, bar and all, put them on his shoulders, and carried them to the top of the hill that faces Hebron.'*

Judges 16:1-3

Can you see it? Well, buckle up your seat belts! The Bible says that, 'a harlot is a deep pit' (1), and that satan shall be, 'brought down to hell, to the sides of the pit' (2). So the scene is one of Jesus entering the stronghold of hell after His death (Gaza means 'a stronghold'). Next, note that these verses record twice that Samson was there, 'all night'. Though, for Samson, this event all happens in one night, the Holy Spirit has deliberately chosen to document two 'nights' before the turning point of 'midnight' arrives. In doing so, Samson previews Jesus' stay in hell. At midnight he 'arises' or better stated, is 'resurrected'. At which point he carries the gates, gateposts, and the locking bar of the stronghold all the way to Hebron (Hebrew: Hebron = Association), which, by the way, is 35 miles away! Here we see the complete humiliation of satan as Jesus carries the gates of hell back to the right hand of His Father's throne in heaven! The bar of the gate speaks of hell's authority to hold people which is, now, totally dismantled through the righteous sacrifice of Jesus for our sin. The gateposts are representative of hell and death (3). Hence, Jesus' declaration to Peter that it is on the revelation of Christ as the Rock on which the church would be built. He rams home our authority when He says, 'THE GATES OF HELL SHALL NOT PREVAIL AGAINST IT' (4), and that He is in possession of its keys (5)!

(1) A masculine noun meaning 'consecrated one', 'devotee' or 'separated'. The term Nazarite means one who is consecrated to God. The Nazarite vow included abstinence from strong drink or the cutting of his hair, and no contact with dead bodies. Samuel and Samson were both Nazarites (Numbers 6; Judges 13:5-7; 16:17; Amos 2:11, 12).

(2) The word is used of Joseph in being separated from his brothers (Genesis 49:26).

(3) An untrimmed vine (Leviticus 25:5).

(4) Separated unto God.

(5) Was Jesus a type of Nazarite? Jesus, the Vine (John 15:1), separated from family. His brothers did not believe in Him (John 7:5).They thought He was out of His mind (Mark 3:21).Here are my brothers, mother, etc. (Matthew 12:47-50; Mark 3:32-35). Does He drink wine? (John 2); Last supper? It is not recorded! He rejected the vinegar! (Matthew 27:34) and declared *'it is finished'* on receiving the vinegar - was he ending his vow?

(1) Proverbs 23:27. (2) Proverbs 2:16,18-19; Isaiah 14:15 cf. Ezekiel 31:16. (3) Revelation 1:18. (4) Matthew 16:18. (5) Revelation 1:18.

Having identified the centerpiece of the gospel in the record of Samson's life it comes as no surprise to discover that his name means, 'Bright Sun' which is in accordance with a title Malachi uses of Jesus,

> *'But unto you that fear my name shall the Sun of righteousness arise with healing in his wings....'*

Malachi 4:2 (KJV)

Samson having been consecrated to the Lord before his birth as a Nazarite, is identified as an 'untrimmed vine' (1) (c). A cursory scan further reveals that it is decreed he would 'begin' to deliver Israel (2), sought a Gentile bride (3), visited her in the time of the wheat harvest (4), uses parables (5), is betrayed for money (6), and, in having the seven locks of hair cut from his head, he is effectively laying down his authority founded in the 7 Spirits of God (7).

(c) Nazarite (H5139) Naziyr. (See note 1 on previous page)

(d) Lion: kepiyr (H3715) from 3722; a village (as covered in by walls); also a lion (as covered with a mane): lion, village. Tenakh has 'full grown lion'.

Defeating a Lion

So having established the landscape between Samson and Christ let's fill out the picture and garner what is rightly ours in the process. We will sidestep an exploration of his consecration as a Nazarite and focus on the incident with a lion. Samson kills no Philistines until he has first dispatched a lion that comes roaring against him (8). Our modern Bibles say that he was a 'young' lion. However, the Hebrew, describes him as a 'kepiyr' lion, that is a lion with a mane which should be better interpreted, 'a full-grown' lion (d). This scene depicts satan, who is elsewhere described like a roaring lion (9) challenging Jesus in the wilderness for dominion of the pride (Israel). The basis on which satan comes and challenges anyone is revealed in Samson's sequel visit to his wife, where, on turning aside to view the carcass of the lion, he discovers a swarm of bees and

(1) cf John 15:1. (2) Judges 13:5; cf. Acts 1:1. (3) Judges 14:1-2. (4) Judges 15:1; cf. John 4:35ff. (5) Judges 14:14; cf. Matthew 13:34 (6) Judges 16:5; cf. Matthew 26:15. (7) Judges 16:17, 19; cf. Isaiah 11:2 . (8) Judges 14:5. (9) 1 Peter 5:8.

honey within. Samson takes some of the honey in his hands and walks on, eating it (1). Honey speaks of receiving revelation and the Spirit of Understanding (2). Samson uses this incident to pose a riddle to the unbelievers in his midst, when he says,

> *'Out of the eater came something to eat,*
> *And out of the strong came something sweet.'*

Judges 14:14

On an elementary level this parable seems to simply be using poetic language to encode drawing honey from the lion. However, on a deeper level, it declares that the lion (satan) accuses us by using the strength of the Law (that which reveals sin and condemns us) to devour us and maintain his dominion (3). When Samson pulls the lion apart, it means that Jesus dismantled the power of satan and the Law to contain and restrict us. Drawing honey from its framework and walking while eating it, speaks of living by faith out of the revelation that is received from it (4).

How important is this? Samson doesn't have dominion over the Philistines without first defeating this lion! Who are the Philistines? The Philistines are unseen entities in Delilah's testing of Samson (5). They are those who seek to intimidate the army of God (6), and they are the same force encamped around the provision of heaven to stop King David drawing water from the well of Bethlehem (7). In short, they are representative of spiritual hosts of wickedness in the heavenly places (8), who seek to impoverish God's people. This explains the centrality of Samson's defeat of a thousand of their number. It is a picture of Christ making an open show in defeating principalities and powers in the heavenlies at the cross (9).

In presenting this parable to the Philistines, Samson pledges 30 changes of clothing if they can understand it (10). Why? The

---

(1) Judges 14:9. (2) cf. 1 Samuel 14:27; Ephesians 1:18; Isaiah 11:2. (3) 1 Corinthians 15:56. (4) Deuteronomy 8:3; 2 Corinthians 5:7. (5) Judges 16:9, 12. (6) 1 Samuel 17:10-11. (7) 2 Samuel 23:14-15. (8) Ephesians 6:12. (9) Colossians 2:15. (10) Judges 14:12.

number thirty is associated with the right time to reign (e). The linen garments described in the wager are those worn by royalty. An understanding of the riddle identifies those who are rightly adorned for rulership because they understand (honey) the voice of God's Spirit through revelation and act (walk) on it (1).

300 Foxes

The next major incident in Samson's life is when he captures 300 foxes, ties them in pairs, and sets them loose with a burning firebrand in their tails (2). You may have asked yourself, 'What is that all about?' To appreciate the significance of the 300 foxes, we have to understand the meaning behind his interrupted marriage to the Timnite (3), Samson releases the burning foxes in response to his father-in-law's act of marrying his wife off to another man. There are a number of indicators that combine to give significance to his intended marriage to the woman from Timnath. It should be acknowledged that the marriage was ordained of God (4), and also that Samson ended up having to give the 30 changes of garments to the Philistines from the turn of events in the marriage pledge. Feeding into this is the meaning in scripture of the number '300', 'foxes' and 'fire'. And finally, when Samson brings down the house of the god of the Philistines as his final act of vengeance, we should note that he does so for his '*two eyes*' (5).

In chapter 4 it was explained that 300 can represent the glory of God. Three hundred in scripture can actually represent the glory of God or the glory of man (f).

Knowing that God often uses 'personification' as a poetic means to address countries and cities (6), we can look beyond what is physically taking place, look into the Spirit realm (7), and discern what is really happening here. The Holy Spirit draws

(e) 30 as 'The right time to reign': how old was Joseph when he came to power? (Genesis 41:46); David? (2 Samuel 5:4); Jesus? (Luke 3:23, cf. Numbers 4:3).

(f) 300 as glory of God or glory of man. When Solomon was king of Israel he had 300 golden shields made and had them housed in the House of the Forest of Lebanon (1 Kings 10:17). These golden shields were a symbol of his glorious kingdom. Five years after Solomon's son, Rehoboam, came to the throne, these golden shields were taken as booty by Shishak king of Egypt. In an attempt to maintain the appearance of the former glorious kingdom Rehoboam had 300 brass shields made in their place (1 Kings 14:25-28). However, the trouble with brass is that it tarnishes and has to constantly be maintained. In contrast to the golden shields the 300 brass shields are symbolic of the glory of men that quickly fades and is but a facade of the real thing.

(1) Romans 8:14. (2) Judges 15:4-5. (3) Judges 14:19-15:2. (4) Judges 14:4. (5) Judges 16:28. (6) Isaiah 23:12; 37:22; 47:1, 8; 54:4. (7) Revelation 1:10.

our attention to the fact that when Samson takes revenge for his two eyes (a gesture of incredible spiritual significance) He is not merely talking about Samson's physical eyes. We are probably being treated to a key to unlock the whole narrative, as, '*the eyes of our understanding are enlightened*' (1). With this in mind, do we find that God makes reference to countries or cities in terms of 'eyes', as in, 'the apple of His eye'? An 'apple' in scripture, in contrast to what most wrongly assume is a symbol of temptation, is actually a token of love (2). So, 'the apple of God's eye' speaks of that which He loves and has His heart set upon. It just so happens that there are two references - one to a country and one to a city - where He does just that. In reference to Israel, Moses records, '*He kept him as the apple of His eye*' (3), and then, in reference to Jerusalem, Zechariah writes, '*for he that touches you touches the apple of His eye*' (4). Wow! In setting his affection upon the Timnite and subsequently Delilah, Samson is foreshadowing Christ's love for Israel and Zion! Delilah means, 'delicate', and rather coincidentally Jeremiah tells us,

> '*I have likened the daughter of Zion*
> *To a lovely and <u>delicate woman</u>.*'

Jeremiah 6:2

Ok, let's quickly put this together: Christ was betrothed to Israel, only she was led astray by her leadership (the Timnite's father) and beguiled by unseen spiritual forces (Philistines). Consequently, her place enthroned upon the nations (30 garments) was taken from her because of her unfaithfulness. In response, God judged Philistia (the fire), because of Israel's leadership (foxes), which sought superficial glory apart from God (300), spoiling the vine (5), and leading Israel into ruin (6).

---

(1) Ephesians 1:19. (2) Song of Songs 2:5. (3) Deuteronomy 32:10. (4) Zechariah 2:8. (5) Song of Songs 2:15. (6) Lamentations 5:18.

Betrayal by Judah

This incident then led Samson into betrayal by 3000 men of Judah (1). A thousand, as we have explained, is representative of a nation and the three in this context means 'chosen, select, leadership', as in Jesus' teaching, *'For many are called, but few are chosen'* (2). The 3000 men of Judah are representative of Judah's spiritual leadership, who handed Jesus over to spiritual hosts of wickedness who used the Romans as hand puppets in the execution process. Samson kills a thousand of their number with the jawbone of an ass, representing Christ's total victory over His accusers at the cross. They thought they had Him nailed as a, 'dead ass' but in fact, God's righteous Servant was very much alive and tore them apart with the very word they tried to use against Him.

Delilah

The Scriptural record then documents Samson's sojourn in Gaza (3), which, as we have discussed, outlines Jesus' journey to hell. Following this, Christ's visit to Jerusalem is foreshadowed through the life of Samson, with the words, *'...he loved a woman in the Valley of Sorek, whose name was Delilah'* (4) (g). Almost instantly the Philistines are at her door asking her to entice him and find out where his strength lies. This is a parallel of the chief priests and elders confronting Jesus about where He gained His authority (5). The interplay that follows in Samson's and Delilah's one-sided love affair echoes Christ's words,

(g) Sorek: (H7796) so'-rek, nachal soreq, 'the valley of the choice vine'.

> *'O Jerusalem, Jerusalem, the one who kills the prophets and stones those who are sent to her! How often I wanted to gather your children together, as a hen gathers her chicks under her wings, but you were not willing!'*
>
> Matthew 23:37

(1) Judges 15:11-13. (2) Matthew 20:16; 22:14. (3) Judges 16:1-3. (4) Judges 16:4. (5) Matthew 21:23.

With armed Philistines waiting in the wings, Delilah tests Samson three times to learn the secret to his strength and how he may be bound (1). This corresponds exactly to the three attempts made by the leadership of Jerusalem to entangle Jesus in His words (2).

The parallel between the two accounts emphasises that binding and loosing (3) is a spiritual faculty based on words. It is also evident, at least from these accounts, that the primary words the enemy jumps upon to accuse and bind us, are our own (4). This emphasises the importance of agreeing with our adversary on the way to the Judge (5) (h), followed by confession that we may be forgiven (6), so that, like Isaiah, a coal from the altar will be placed on our lips declaring us clean (7). Just as the Philistines would have taken the opportunity to do Samson harm had he not broken free from Delilah's superficial bonds, so the enemy also seizes on those occasions where words are 'thrown over us' by others. These also need to be broken off by recognizing them, renouncing them and replacing them with what God says about us (i).

The following testimony which comes from my good friend Jim Freiberg in Denver, Colorado, is testament to the enemy's ability to use our words against us.

'I was in the construction field as a project manager and later as a director of construction for 30-plus years when I was laid off by my company. It was a humbling experience. In retrospect, I believe that the Lord had break-through for us all along, but the enemy used my own words against me. I used to say things like "I will never go back into the construction industry, its dead". Once I realized what I had consistently been speaking over my life, I repented and asked the Lord to forgive me. My wife and I immediately went to a little mountain top not too far from our home and declared the promises of God

(h) If we are guilty of wrong confession.

(i) See masseuse dream chapter 6 page 73.

(1) Judges 16:6-9, 10-12, 13-14. (2) Matthew 22:15-22, 23-33, 34-46. (3) Matthew 16:19. (4) Matthew 12:37. (5) Matthew 5:25. (6) 1 John 1:9. (7) Isaiah 6:5-7.

over our life. The very next day I had two job offers! Over the course of the two year layoff, I probably sent out 300 resumes and I maybe received two phone calls back, no interviews. So today, I more fully understand that with every word that I speak I am either building up or tearing down, I don't always get it right but I do know when I speak wrongly and quickly correct myself.'

The Bible says that Delilah pressed Samson, '*to the point of death*' with her words (1). Subsequently, he effectively lays his life down for her in revealing his lifelong secret; that the seven locks of his head are the key to his strength. Those seven locks of hair represent the seven Spirits of God with which he and Christ were endowed, and in which Samson's strength and Christ's authority rested. If you know the story, Delilah seizes upon the information, lulls Samson to sleep and has his head shaven. You may also recall the pitiful scene of Samson standing to his feet, not realizing that the Spirit of the Lord has left him and without the strength to resist his foes (2). What possessed Samson to give up his union with God? It was the love he had for Delilah that was, '*as strong as death*' (3)! It was a scene previously played out in Adam's love for Eve (4), and replayed in Christ's love for Israel and given expression at the cross. He too was struck with the enormity of His separation from the Father, causing Him to cry out, '*My God, My God, why have You forsaken me?*' (5). Having launched his ministry with the defeat of a lion, Samson is now a lion without a mane (the symbol of his authority) and powerless to resist (j). That once lion-like figure, now became outwardly pathetic, taking on the semblance of a voiceless 'lamb' before his slaughterers (6) (k).

The story moves to its climax. The Philistines take Samson into captivity and enact physically what had already taken place, spiritually, by poking out his eyes. The enemy thought that it

(j) The Hebrew word Na'ar (H5286) which means to shake (off, out, self) describing a lion shaking himself and standing, arousing himself to defend his pride. Rustling of the lion's mane, which is usually accompanied the lion's roar. This means that Samson's ministry began and concluded with a lion.

(k) He who loved God (Mark 12:30), was now loving mankind (Mark 12:31), with no greater love (John 15:13).

(1) Judges 16:16. (2) Judges 16:17-20. (3) Song of Songs 8:6. (4) 1 Timothy 2:14. (5) Matthew 27:46. (6) Isaiah 53:7.

was all over. However, the Bible says, '*the hair of his head began to grow again*' (1), and the characters are prepared for the final showdown. The lords of the Philistines, drunk with victory, organize a celebration in the temple of dagon, their god, and Samson is paraded as a trophy. It is recorded that there were 3000 in attendance, and like those from Judah who arrested Samson, the Holy Spirit is bringing to our attention that these are the cream of Philistia, gathered, as it were, by invite only. Led to the two pillars that supported the whole structure, Samson prays that in one act he might exact vengeance for his two '*eyes*'. Jesus likewise, in one act, because of His love for Israel and Jerusalem, brings down satan's house built on the two pillars of sin and death! So, like Samson, in death, He totally crushed and annihilated satan's authority (2) to use the law against us. As they had done to him, Samson in turn returned to their own heads (3).

Could it be that Samson deserves our reappraisal? Either the Holy Spirit has recorded his shortcomings so they highlight his parallel with Christ with incredible detail, or he has been totally misunderstood and misrepresented both in his day and since. Indeed, if he acted as an obedient servant - without the hindsight afforded us - following the leading of the Spirit beyond the confines of the law, he rightly deserves both God's commendation, and ours, of being truly worthy to be placed among the heroes of faith (4) (I).

(I) It could be, that like Christ, we are only able to fully appreciate his obedient sacrifice in hindsight.

The Baptism of the Spirit

You may have noticed in following the life of Samson that God was using a form of parallelism in presenting three different accounts of the victory of the cross. The first is documented as the killing of a 1000 Philistines with the jawbone of an ass, the second is his visit to Gaza, and the final one features Delilah

(1) Judges 16:22. (2) Genesis 3:15; Colossians 2:15. (3) Judges 15:11. (4) Hebrews 11:32.

and the temple of dagon. The footage provided by each of these differently angled shots provides more insights into Christ's victory than a single record could hope to capture. Therefore, the life of Samson is unique in its ability to present the absolute completeness of that triumphant day. His life story has effectively presented the total defeat of the enemies of God in all spheres: above the earth, under the earth and on the earth (1).

When Samson defeated the 1000 Philistines with the jawbone of an ass, there is another incident that has not yet been highlighted. At the point when Samson prophetically cries out, '*I thirst!*' (2) (in sync with an event yet to be outplayed on a 'future' stage) it is recorded that he threw the jawbone. Where it landed and struck the earth he called both, '*Ramath Lehi*' and '*En Hakkore*' (3). '*Ramath Lehi*' literally means, 'Jawbone of the Height', which can be interpreted, 'Words from on high', (Mouth of God), and, '*En Hakkore*', happens to mean, 'Spring of the Caller'. Similarly when Jesus died upon the cross, He not only cleansed us of sin, He also opened the Well of heaven so that it may flow through us. What this means is that when we pray in the Spirit, the well within us is opened (4) - the well of the caller - to allow the voice of God to be released through us. In other words, when we pray in tongues, the Spirit of God is speaking through us to meet the spiritual desire or 'thirst' He has placed within!

Grow Your Anointing

In the last of the scenarios presented, where Samson reveals to Delilah how he may be bound, he repeatedly contrasts his strength with becoming weak, '*like any other man*' (5). In contrasting himself to other men, he reveals that it is consecration - a separation unto God - marked by an anointing

(1) Philippians 2:10; Revelation 5:12-13. (2) Judges 15:18. (3) Judges 15:17, 19. (4) John 7:37-39. (5) Judges 16:7, 11, 17.

that separates God's people from others. In light of this understanding, we are mandated to live out of the eternal realm (consecrated to God), and in doing so, our anointing grows. We do well if we value, nurture and protect that anointing.

Prayer:

Father, just as they attempted to bind Samson, and catch Jesus in His words, I realize that the enemy pounces on my words to stop me being all You destined for me. I come before You and admit my negativity and wrong confession in saying...(quote your wrong confession). Please forgive me according to Your word and grant the grace to watch what I say in future. I am a new creation consecrated to live out of the eternal realm. Please place Your spiritual thirst within me to see Your kingdom come on earth. Amen.

Summary:

- Without the insights of the Old Testament we are incapable of truly comprehending the kingdom into which we have been called.

- A higher script is being outplayed in the narrative that documents the life and ministry of Samson.

- Samson's defeat of 1000 Philistines parallels Christ's victory at the cross.

- His visit to Gaza prefigures Christ's visit to hell.

- Samson's ministry begins with the killing of a lion (in parallel with Christ's defeat of satan in the wilderness).

- Samson's defeat of Philistines is representative of Christ's victory over principalities and powers in the spirit realm.

- The episodes with the Timnite and Delilah are representative of God's love for Israel and Jerusalem.

- The narrative of Samson's life is unique in that it portrays the magnitude of Christ's victory on three levels: above the earth, under the earth and on the earth.

- In throwing the jawbone of the ass Samson symbolically portrayed Christ opening heaven's reservoir.

- Praying in the Spirit opens the 'well of the caller' within us releasing God's 'words from on high'.

- We are mandated to live out of the eternal realm (consecrated to God), and in so doing, our anointing (that which separates us from other men) grows.

Chapter 11

The Akedah

Our discussion on Samson highlights the power and importance of establishing context when extracting kingdom realities from the Old Testament. Similarly, our next truth relating to speaking in tongues comes as a follow-on to one of the four mountains (stand-outs in the landscape of the OT) presented in the Tanakh (Jewish OT) of Christ's vicarious sacrifice (1) (a).

(a) 4 Mountain Tops of OT:

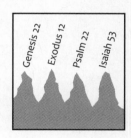

Many will be familiar with the story of Abraham offering up his son (2), an incident that in Judaism is known as the 'Akedah', which means the 'Binding' (of Isaac). However, I have found that many have never had the depth of this passage opened to them. The passage is an absolute treasure trove of revelation.

(1) Genesis 22; Exodus 12; Psalm 22; Isaiah 53. (2) Genesis 22.

The Journey to the Mount

This episode is considered the tenth and final test of Abraham, the father of the faith. It begins with God commanding Abraham to take his son, and *'go to'* the land of Moriah. Here he is to sacrifice Isaac as a burnt offering unto the Lord, on a mountain that will be shown him (1). A burnt offering was a voluntary offering up of an animal or fowl that made the offerer acceptable before God (2). In using the directive, *'go to'* (Hebrew: 'lekh-lekha'), the Holy Spirit is directing our attention back to Abraham's initial call to leave his own country, where, in the Hebrew, he was told to do the same (3) (b). As such, he is once again shown to be moving by faith. At this point it is evident that Isaac is described with increasing personal definition, *'Your son, your only son, Isaac whom you love'* (4). This not only parallels the progressive personalized ownership of the Passover lamb from, *'a lamb'*, *'the lamb'*, to, *'Your lamb'* (5), it also echoes the personal titles of Jesus as the, *'Only begotten'* (6), and *'beloved Son'* (7).

The Bible then records that, *'On the third day Abraham lifted his eyes and saw the place afar off'* (8). At this point, we need to ask, 'How long was the son dead in the father's heart'? Answer: three days (9). It is also worthy of note that in, *'lifting his eyes'* reference is being made beyond the natural scene, to suggest Abraham is seeing in the Spirit the destiny that awaits Christ.

Abraham then directs his servants to stay at the base of the mount with the ass, while he and Isaac go up to worship (10) (c). This is the first mention of *'worship'* in scripture. What a revelation. True worship is not a slow song, but a sacrifice of one's life. He then completes his instruction to his servants by saying, *'and we will come back to you'*, which speaks of his belief in a resurrection (11).

(b) cf. Genesis 12:1b *'I will show you'*.

(c) Mount Moriah is later recorded as the place upon which Solomon built the Temple (Genesis 22:2; 2 Chronicles 3:1).

(1) Genesis 22:1-2. (2) Leviticus 1; 6:9-12. (3) Genesis 12:1. (4) Genesis 22:2.
(5) Exodus 12:3-5. (6) John 3:16. (7) Matthew 3:17. (8) Genesis 22:4.
(9) cf. Mark 8:31; 9:31; 10:34; Luke 24:7, 21, 46; John 2:19; Acts 10:39-40.
(10) Genesis 22:5. (11) Genesis 22:5.

Isaac carries the wood on his back up the mount, just as Jesus was made to carry the cross to Golgotha (1). Isaac asks, *'Where is the lamb for a burnt offering?'* To which Abraham responds, *'God will provide, Himself, the Lamb, for burnt offering'* (2). Although Isaac was earlier described as a *'lad'* (3), most rabbinic commentators see him as an adult, and thus in stating, *'So the two of them went together'* (4), we know that Isaac was a willing participant in his own sacrifice.

Having built the altar Abraham puts the wood *'in order'* before *'binding'* his son and placing him upon it (5). The cross, of course, is wood, *'prepared'* or *'put in order'*, and *'binding'*, as was discovered in the previous chapter, refers to 'words' or 'accusations' holding one in preparation for judgment. When Abraham lifts the *'knife'*, which speaks of words of judgment being meted out (6) (d). God intervenes and stops him, and provides, *'behind him...a ram caught by his horns in a thicket'*, as a substitute (7). The Hebrew word *'behind'* is also elsewhere translated, *'afterwards'*. Afterwards, Jesus was laid upon the cross as our substitute (8). The words of accusation were not able to hold Him (9), He lay down His authority/strength (horns), wore a crown of thorns (10), and died in our place (11).

(d) Knife as judgment: Proverbs 30:14; Hebrews 4:12.

It is to be noted that the Bible records, *'So Abraham returned to his young men, and they rose and went...'* (12). There is no mention of Isaac, though he is obviously among them. The Holy Spirit has deliberately left mention of him out to complete the picture of Jesus dying upon the cross.

Finally, as a result of his unflinching obedience, Abraham is promised that his, *'seed shall possess the gate of his enemies'* (13), which was also fully implemented in Jesus' death upon the cross and subsequent victory over hell and death.

There is so much more, but what has been displayed above confirms that the Akedah is a indisputable prequel to the main

(1) John 19:17. (2) Genesis 22:7-8. (3) Genesis 22:5. (4) Genesis 22:8.
(5) Genesis 22:9. (6) Genesis 22:10. (7) Genesis 22:13. (8) John 1:29.
(9) Acts 2:24, 27. (10) John 19:2. (11) Colossians 1:22; 2 Corinthians 5:15, 21.
(12) Genesis 22:19. (13) Genesis 22:17; cf. Galatians 3:16.

event outplayed in the Gospels. Now, given that foreground, let us focus on the rest of the picture.

Securing a Bride

The following chapter (1), tells the story of Sarah's death and of Abraham's need to purchase a burial site in the land, where he is a 'resident alien' without hereditary land rights, despite being promised the whole land (2). Abraham purchases a burial site for Sarah and secures a legal right for his offspring.

Abraham now commissions his servant to seek a bride for his son, Isaac (3). Encompassing the servant's quest are two repeated lines of poetic scripture which alert the reader to the link between Akedah and this event (e). The poetic bond is the promise given to Abraham's seed of '*possessing the gate of his enemies*' (4), which is also pronounced upon Rebekah by her family when she decides to follow the servant back to Isaac (5).

The narrative commenced with Abraham commissioning his servant to bring a bride for Isaac, his son, from the land of his family (6). Abraham promises that God will send His angel ahead of the servant to ensure success (7). Abraham is adamant that the servant is not to take Isaac back to that place, but that the intended bride is to come to his son (8). The servant takes ten of his master's camels loaded with '*goods*' (f), and heads for the city of Nahor (Abraham's relative), in Mesopotamia (9). On arrival he gets his camels to kneel before the well of the city and prays as the women come from the city to draw water from the well (10). He asks for a confirmation of his success, by praying,

> '...*the young woman to whom I say, "Please let down your pitcher that I may drink," and she says, "Drink, and I will also give you camels a drink"- let her be the one You have appointed for Your servant Isaac.*'
>
> Genesis 24:14

(e) An example of inclusion. See chapter 8 page 102.

(f) Goods: (H2898) tûb: A masculine noun meaning property, goods, goodness, fairness, and beauty. The root concept of this noun is that of desirability for enjoyment.

(1) Genesis 23 (2) Genesis 13:14-15, 17; 15:7; Psalm 105:42, 44. (3) Genesis 24. (4) Genesis 22:17. (5) Genesis 24:60. (6) Genesis 24:2-4. (7) Genesis 24:7. (8) Genesis 24:6. (9) Genesis 24:10. (10) Genesis 24:11-13.

Even before he has finished praying, Rebekah comes on the scene. When she has filled her pitcher with water, Abraham's servant requests a little of it (1). Rebekah lets down her vase and when he has finished drinking, almost on cue, she volunteers to water his camels. (2). On discovering that she is Abraham's relative (3), the servant takes from his provisions a golden nose ring (or earring) and two golden bands (or bracelets) for her arms (4). The servant is taken to her mother's home where he recounts both the nature of his mission and the favor of God upon his quest. The servant worships at the recognition of God's hand in the meeting process (5), and again at the approval of the proposal by Rebekah and her family (6). The witness of the servant's story, the report of his master's good fortune, and the down payment of gifts, is enough to convince Rebekah to go with the servant. On her departure Rebekah's family pronounce a blessing that she become, '*the mother of thousands and ten thousands*', and as mentioned, that, her '*seed would possess the gate of her enemies*' (7). The story comes to a close with Rebekah meeting Isaac face to face near the well Lahai Roi (8).

The Bride is wooed by:

-The Good News
-The Witness of the Servant
- A display of the Gifts

I suggest, that this longest chapter in the Book of Genesis parallels the longest Book in the New Testament, the Book of Acts. What we are seeing outplayed here, following the indisputable portrayal of Christ's death at Golgotha, is the same commissioning of the Holy Spirit to gather a Gentile bride, the Church, to be united with Christ (9).

This passage deliberately does not reveal the name of the servant because he is a forerunner of the 'Unnamed Servant', the Holy Spirit (10). However, most rabbinic scholars take him to be Abraham's senior steward, '*Eliezer*' (11), which, without coincidence, means, 'Helper'.

In accordance with Abraham's recognition that God's angel will go before Eliezer, the New Testament tells us that angels

(1) Genesis 24:15-17. (2) Genesis 24:18-19. (3) Genesis 24:47. (4) Genesis 24:22. (5) Genesis 24:26-27, 48. (6) Genesis 24:52. (7) Genesis 24:60. (8) Genesis 24:61-65. (9) John 16:7. (10) John 16:13. (11) Genesis 15:2.

are, '*ministering spirits sent forth to minister for those who will inherit salvation*' (1). The firmness with which Abraham warns the servant not to take his son to the place of his origin, is a caution that the Body of Christ should not be enveloped in the world, but that the Church should instead be gathered out of the world (2).

Is it possible that, apart from the one Eliezer is riding, the other nine gift-laden camels represent the nine gifts of the Spirit (g)? And that when these camels kneel before the well we have a picture of humble servants awaiting the release of the gifts of the Spirit before the well of heaven?

Eliezer displays the thankfulness and attitude of worship pivotal to the success of the mission, a mission for which we too have been commissioned. As agents of God, the same heart attitude releases the gifts through us as pure conduits, bearing witness of His handiwork to confirm the testimony we bring.

The bride-to-be receives a golden earring, signifying entry to a new relationship of faith (3) (h), and two golden arm bands, representing the union of man and God in the work to be accomplished (4).

Rebekah returns with the servant on the basis of his testimony, the good news of Isaac's prosperity (5) and the witness of the gifts. Likewise, the Church is gathered on the good news of the gospel of the kingdom, the witness of the Holy Spirit and the display of the gifts.

In the Genesis record there is no mention of Isaac, between his figurative departure on Mount Moriah (6) until he meets his bride (7). It is a picture of Christ enthroned in heaven awaiting the revealing of His Bride. The story comes to a close with Rebekah being brought to Isaac, who is meditating at the well

(g) It is later revealed that Eliezer is accompanied (Genesis 24:32, 54).

(h) The earring in Exodus 21:5-6 conveys that the servant now has ears for his master. Rebekah is similarly given an earring or nose ring signifying entry to a new level of spiritual guidance paralleling sensory guidance: smell or hearing (faith) (cf. Romans 10:17).

(1) Hebrews 1:14. (2) John 8:23; 15:19; 17:14, 16. (3) Romans 10:17. (4) Ephesians 2:10. (5) Genesis 24:36. (6) Genesis 22:19. (7) Genesis 24.

Lahai Roi. Lahai Roi is variously translated as the well of 'the One Who Lives and Sees Me', 'well of the living One who sees', and 'the Well of Living Water' (A). The Body of Christ is likewise to be found murmuring (meditating) forth the Living Water of heaven's supply to a dry and thirsting world (1).

When did the Servant Dispense Gifts?

The crucial point from all of this, is that the gifts of the Spirit were not distributed until Rebekah had a willingness to draw water. The scene is representative of the need to speak in tongues, bringing forth living water so that the Spirit can then move upon us with the gifts. On the Day of Pentecost it was not prophecy, healings or even miracles that first marked the outpouring of the Spirit. The outpouring of the Spirit was ushered in by tongues of fire and speaking in tongues (2). The fire speaks of the consecration of the vessel and the tongues act as the channel to bring in whatever God wills through the gifts. This is why the Apostle Paul writes,

'But now, brethren, if I come to you speaking with tongues, what shall I profit you unless I speak to you either by revelation, by knowledge, by prophesying, or by teaching?'

1 Corinthians 14:6

In context, Paul is explaining that tongues are not an end in themselves, their purpose is more important than their manifestation. He is alluding to the fact that they are the catalyst for what follows. They release it, they empower it. We are not to be caught up with their outward display, but with what they release in the Spirit.

Redigging Wells

Why is it that tongues is such a contentious issue amongst

(1) John 7:37-39. (2) Acts 2:3-4.

Christians? I heard of one large church in the Midwest that documents its opposition to this expression of the Spirit by including a denial of speaking in tongues in the church charter which is displayed in the foyer! Would you like to see that in the Torah?

There is an incident, after Abraham's death, where in a time of famine, Isaac was instructed by God not to go to Egypt (the world) but to remain in Gerar among the Philistines (1). In fear, Isaac, like his father before him, lies about the status of Rebekah, saying that she is his sister and not his wife (2). Regardless of this indiscretion, God blesses and prospers him, and as a consequence the Philistines envied him (3) and forced his departure from their midst (4). Then the Philistines stopped up with earth all the wells which Abraham had dug (5). Isn't it interesting that following an act of the flesh - lying because of fear - the wells are also blocked with earth (which also represents the flesh)? It is pretty simple really, when we are in the flesh we are not in the Spirit. The enemy's tactics have not changed. If he can intimidate us with fear to live only on this level of 'reality', he can block up our well with earth to stop us drawing refreshing life from a deeper, eternal level called 'truth'. Therefore, a church that legislates - whether deliberately or ignorantly - against speaking in tongues is a church content to live at a lower level.

Isaac is forced to relocate and redig the wells the Philistines have stopped up. Significantly, he renames the wells by the same name his father had called them (6). It is no coincidence that today, over and over, progressive generations of Christian movements lose the impetus of their founders when they stray from the Spirit that birthed them. In restoring the names Abraham used, there are three truths revealed. Firstly, every generation needs a fresh revelation of the need of the Baptism

(1) Genesis 26:1-6. (2) Genesis 26: 7-11. (3) Genesis 26:12-14. (4) Genesis 26:16. (5) Genesis 26:15. (6) Genesis 26:18.

of the Spirit. Secondly, we are not likely to bother to dig afresh in God without a level of pressure upon us, and finally, there will be contention over each progressive outpouring before it is accepted and room is made for it (1).

Moses' Failure to Enter

Jesus came to give us salvation and with it the Promise of the Father - the outpouring of the Holy Spirit - the river of Life from heaven (living water) bringing His life source to a dry world (2). However, it is one thing to get saved and delivered from Egypt, it is quite another to cross Jordan and enter the Promised Land. Just ask those who died in the wilderness!

> **Who Am I?**
>
> I was a controversial NT believer
> Like Israel, I was humbled in the wilderness
> My life and teaching endorsed the Ancient Paths
> I revealed the new creation is faith working through love.
>
> Answer: Page 183 ff.

Early in the wilderness experience Moses encountered a rock. Needing water to quench Israel's thirst he was commanded to strike the rock (3). God explained that He would stand before Moses on the rock, and then directed him to strike the rock. In striking it, Moses was figuratively enacting what took place at the cross of Calvary. As he struck the rock with the rod he was symbolically judging Christ, and the result was an outflow of water as heaven opened. At the closing of his journey through the wilderness Moses again encountered a rock when Israel needed water. This time Moses was commanded to '*speak*' to the rock and was assured that it would again bring forth water (4). Instead of speaking to it, he struck the rock as before (5), and, as a consequence, was not permitted to enter the Promised Land (6). In striking the rock, Moses was figuratively stuck at the cross crucifying Christ a second time. Salvation is one thing, entry into the Promised Land is quite another.

The gift of speaking in tongues is the channel for the rest

(1) Genesis 26:18, 20-22. (2) Luke 24:49; Acts 1:4. (3) Exodus 17:6. (4) Numbers 20:8. (5) Numbers 20:11. (6) Numbers 20:12.

of the gifts (1). It has the ability to deliver God's payload from heaven and move the Body of Christ into the realm of the manifestation of His promises. It is little wonder the devil and his demons (Philistines) take great delight in stirring religious earthbound dwellers to oppose its expression.

> *'You have to understand, most of these people are not ready to be unplugged. And many of them are so inert, so hopelessly dependent on the system that they will fight to protect it.'*

Morpheus (The Matrix)

(1) 1 Corinthians 12:7-10.
(A) Missler, p. 67, *Genesis Expositional Commentary*, 1995, Koinonia House Inc.

Prayer:

Father, I thank You that angels are sent ahead of me to those who will inherit salvation. I also understand that in saying *'Your seed shall possess the gate of his enemies'* that Your word in me dispossesses satan's authority. Therefore, in the area of my finances, relationships, workplace and family, etc. I proclaim the promises You have given me (quote those promises). I declare that, according to Your word, satan must relinquish his authority over those areas and they are now under the kingdom reign of God, with all His associated blessings. Amen.

Summary:

- The Akedah is a powerful parallel of Christ's sacrificial offering at Calvary.

- In commissioning his 'unnamed' servant to bring a bride for his son, Abraham foreshadows the Holy Spirit being sent to gather the church.

- The bride returns with the servant based on the servant's witness, the good report and a display of the gifts.

- Rebekah demonstrates that bringing forth water releases the gifts just as speaking in tongues does.

- Speaking in tongues is the catalyst for the gifts.

- The devil attempts to intimidate us to live out of this world's level of reality, to block our well and stop us from drawing life-giving water from the eternal realm.

- Isaac's need to redig the wells his father had dug reveals that:

  - every generation needs a fresh revelation of the Baptism of the Spirit.
  - we need pressure to pursue the Baptism.
  - there will be contention over each progressive outpouring of the Spirit.

- Moses' two encounters with rocks in the wilderness metaphorically shows that salvation is one thing, entering the Promised Land is quite another.

Chapter 12

The Trumpets

Our discussions so far confirm the mystic tenet that there are indeed layers of truth hidden within the scriptures. From our earlier explorations of Babel, Moses, the Akedah, Isaac's wells, Hannah's prayer, and episodes from the life of Samson, it can also be seen that speaking in tongues is a much more important gift, than has been realized by the Church. There is one other key symbol in the Old Testament representative of singing in tongues, that I would now like to highlight.

Just as a well and the water flowing from it is symbolic of a refreshing flow of words through a cleft to a dry and parched people (1), so a trumpet is an aperture through which the breath of the musician's spirit is amplified to make declarations in the heavenly realms.

In Biblical Israel there were two types of trumpets - the shofar and the silver trumpet - which were thought of as

(1) John 7:37-38; Ephesians 5:26.

signalling instruments in religious and secular ceremonies. However, the Bible actually teaches that both types of trumpet are a voice (1),

> *'With trumpets and sound (voice) of cornet (the shofar) make a joyful noise before the Lord, the King.'*

> Psalms 98:6 (KJV)

Two silver trumpets were used for the calling of the assembly and for the journeying of the camps. They were also used to sound an alarm in times of war, so that Israel would be remembered before the Lord and saved from their enemies (2). At the beginning of months, silver trumpets were blown over offerings as a memorial before the Lord (3).

The shofar, 'sopar', is a ram's horn. It's name appears to have been adopted from the Akkadian version of the Sumerian word for the 'wild goat'. The shofar is sounded every Friday night to begin the Sabbath, it is blown to announce the seventh month (Tishri), which is marked by the Feast of Trumpets (4), and its blasts also declare the Year of Jubilee (5). Each of the occasions signify the entry of 'Rest'. When the shofar is blown on Rosh Hashanah (a) it is seen as a declaration of God's promise to Abraham, Isaac and Jacob and is powerfully linked to the ram that was Isaac's substitute,

(a) The shofar (sopar) was essentially a signalling instrument, especially in times of war. It was used as a call to arms (Judges 3:27; 6:34; Nehemiah 4:18-20), it was also used as a warning alarm (Jeremiah 6:1; Ezekiel 33:3-6; Hosea 5:8), a retreat (2 Samuel 18:16), a proclamation of victory (1 Samuel 13:3), the disbanding of forces (2 Samuel 20:1, 22). Its voice alarmed and frightened the enemy (Judges 4:19-21), it heralded the year of Jubilee (Leviticus 25:9, 13), and proclaimed the Day of Atonement (Yom Kippur) (Leviticus 23:26-32; 25:9; Exodus 30:10).

> *'That in blessing I will bless you, and in multiplying I will multiply your seed as the stars of the heaven, and as the sand which is upon the sea shore; and your seed shall possess the gate of his enemies.'*

> Genesis 22:17 (KJV Modernized)

Symbolically an animal's horns represent its strength. It is the point through which the entire power of the beast can be

(1) cf. Exodus 19:16, 19; Revelation 1:10; 4:1. (2) Numbers 10:1-2. (3) Numbers 10:9-10. (4) Leviticus 23:24. (5) Leviticus 25:9.

exerted. So the ram that found itself caught in a thicket and was offered as a burnt offering, prefigures Christ laying down His authority and taking on the curse of the law (thorns), so that we would be blessed (1) (b). In this context, the sound of the shofar represents the entry into His 'Rest' (2), and the authoritative Word of God invoking and declaring that promise over the household of faith.

(b) New Year's Day: 1st Tishri Feast of Trumpets (Rosh Hashanah) (Leviticus 23:24, 25) day of blowing trumpets to begin Civil New Year.

So it is that the scriptures link the Presence of the Spirit with trumpets,

> *'...the Spirit of the Lord came upon Gideon,*
> *and he blew a trumpet....'*

> Judges 6:34 (KJV)

And knowing that the sound of a trumpet is as a voice,

> *'I was in the Spirit on the Lord's Day,*
> *and I heard behind me a loud voice, as of a trumpet.'*

> Revelation 1:10

Though this verse primarily addresses the authority or volume of the voice, it also teaches that what may sound like an indiscernible trumpet is, in the Spirit, understood as a recognized voice (3). It is reasonable to say, that when we are singing in the Spirit our voice is as a trumpet. It is not surprising that in bringing order to the Corinthian church in the operation of tongues and interpretation, the Apostle Paul links trumpets and tongues. He says,

> *'For if the trumpet give an uncertain sound,*
> *who will prepare for battle?'*

> 1 Corinthians 14:8

This understanding then, helps us reassess Nehemiah's

(1) Genesis 22:13. (2) Hebrews 4:3-4. (3) cf. John 12:28-29; Exodus 19:19.

comment while rebuilding the walls of Jerusalem. He simply says,

'And he that sounded the trumpet was by me.'

Nehemiah 4:18 (KJV)

The trumpeter represents the Spirit of God. There is obviously more going on here than meets the eye. Two verses later, Nehemiah declares,

'Wherever you hear the sound of the trumpet,
rally to us there. Our God will fight for us.'

Nehemiah 4:20

In blowing the trumpet God's army of angels are mustered. They fight the unseen spirit battle that is behind any earthly conflict (1). When Gideon's 300 men blew their shofars God's angels, which accompany the son's of God (2), went to work and brought confusion into the enemy's ranks. It was like a scene from a movie with thousands of computer-generated extras! Victory was rightly attributed to their Commander,

'And the three hundred blew the trumpets, and the Lord set
every man's sword against his fellow,
even throughout all the host....'

Judges 7:22 (KJV)

Jericho

Given that we do not always carry around with us our shofars, and recognizing that trumpets and tongues are interchangeable between Testaments, we should look afresh at Israel's most critical battle in which the shofar was the pre-eminent weapon.

(1) Ephesians 6:12. (2) 2 Samuel 5:24.

The Battle Viewed from Earth

God's battle plan for Jericho was for the men of war to circle around the city once for six days. The ark was to be carried preceded by seven priests making blasts on 7 ram's horns (shofars). Men of war were to march before and after the ark (1). On the seventh day the city was to be encircled 7 times, while the priests blew their trumpets continuously (2). Finally, the priests were to make a long blast on their shofars, followed by the rest of the men of war making a great shout, after which the walls would fall down.

It is evident that the ark played a significant role in this ritual-like event as is highlighted by the use of words, '*So the ark of the Lord compassed the city...*' (3). Stripped from all its trimmings, this verse draws our attention to the fact that the ark was the centerpiece of this entourage of solders, priests and trumpets, and to their very precise instructions. During this seven-day exercise the only voices that were to be heard were the seven ram's horns. None of the people were allowed to speak until the time came when they were to shout (4).

It is interesting, given the details of the orders to be followed, that in encompassing the city for seven straight days (breaking the Sabbath), Joshua and his men were violating Mosaic Law (5).

Finally, this passage records that there was to be no booty taken for the people of Israel. The city of Jericho was to be razed to the ground and everything within it, was accursed, or, in Hebrew, 'herem' (devoted to destruction) (6). The only exception to this was that Rahab and her family were to be spared and the city's metals were to be consecrated to the Lord.

Who Am I?

I appear from cover to cover of the Bible
I am embraced before and after the cross
I am as relevant today as I was of old
However, there are many who are unaware I exist
This may be cause for many embarking, but few arriving.

Answer: Chapter 13.

(1) Joshua 6:3-4, 7-9. (2) Joshua 6:4, 13. (3) Joshua 6:11. (4) Joshua 6:10.
(5) Exodus 20:10; 31:14; Leviticus 23:3. (6) Joshua 6:17-19.

The Battle Viewed from Heaven

Joshua's march, Samson's honey and Elijah's ravens tell us that bringing heaven's purposes to earth takes more than obedience to a set of rules. Supernatural outbreaks of the power of God call for an obedience beyond the law. Being led of the Spirit (1) and hearing the Living word of God (2) requires a willingness to step outside, of what is, at times, culturally acceptable. Often, like Abraham offering up his only son (3), we are participants in a scene that is beyond our current understanding and whose eternal purpose may only be realized in hindsight. Joshua and his men entered into just such an opportunity at Jericho.

Having recognized that the ark is central to this episode, we need to ask what does it represent? We would immediately say, 'The Presence of God', and that would be absolutely correct, but there is more to it. We need to identify what was in the ark. There were the two tablets containing the ten commandments, Aaron's rod that budded, and a sample of the manna eaten in the wilderness. What do these represent? The ten commandments represents the law, or the word of God. The rod that budded represents resurrection life and the manna is bread from heaven. Who is the Word of God? Who is the Resurrection and the Life? And, Who is the True Bread from heaven? Jesus is all three (4)! So the ark is a picture of Christ being carried around Jericho. Hold that thought for a moment.

To fully unlock the mystery of Jericho we need to go back to a time when Abram cut covenant with God and was promised that his seed would come into the Land of Canaan after 400 years of oppression in Egypt (5). At that moment the clock starting ticking on Jericho,

(1) Romans 8:14. (2) Deuteronomy 8:3. (3) Genesis 22. (4) John 1:1, 14; 11:25; 6:32-35. (5) Genesis 15:7-18.

*'But in the fourth generation they shall come here again:
for the iniquity of the Amorites is not yet full.'*

Genesis 15:16 (KJV)

Although the two kings defeated by Israel on the east of the Jordan River are identified as being Amorites (1), and the close neighbour of Jericho, Ai, is also reported as being an Amorite stronghold (2), Scripture doesn't directly identify Jericho's heritage, though it may be suggested that it was of Amorite origin (3).

Whether Jericho is technically an Amorite city or not, is not important, because God later makes reference to the Amorites as representative of all the inhabitants of Canaan (4), and similarly classified them all as Hittites when Joshua was about to enter Canaan (5). In that latter situation God made reference to all of its inhabitants as *'Hittites'* because the number one issue confronting Joshua was 'Fear', and the meaning of the word 'Hittite' is 'Affrighted by fear'. That would suggest that God's assessment of Canaan's inhabitants applied to their character. The meaning of the name 'Amorite' means to 'Boast self' and it is quite reasonable to suggest Canaan's inhabitants, which included giants, were characterised by pride. With regard to Jericho, itself, it is evident that a city centrally located in Canaan, with strong nations north and south of it, would need substantial walls as a defence against invaders. These walls could, understandably, become a source of pride (6). The fact that Rahab, whose house was on the wall, had a window through which the two Israelite spies were *'let down'* (7) also suggests substantial height was involved.

So Jericho was circumnavigated for 6 days once, and then 7 times on the seventh day, which is a total of 13 times. Making that journey were the ark and 7 priests bearing 7 shofars. The ark as we have shown represents Jesus Christ, but more

(1) Joshua 2:10. (2) Joshua 7:5, 7. (3) cf. Joshua 24:11. (4) Joshua 24:15.
(5) Joshua 1:4. (6) cf. Proverbs 18:11. (7) Joshua 2:18.

definitively, Jesus as '*the Sun of Righteousness*' (1). Therefore, the ark making its journey around Jericho represents years (revolutions of the sun) from the time of Abram's promise till the day that it was intended God would judge Jericho, as the heart and entry-point of the land. That was not simply 13 years, but rather 13 Jubilees (as indicated by the 7 priests bearing 7 trumpets) or 13 times (7x7) years which equals 637 years. This is 40 years short of the actual 677 years it took Abram's descendants to make that journey (c). Why did they take an extra 40 years? It took an extra 40 years because in unbelief they failed to enter His rest (2), and a new generation had to be raised up to take their place. This 'rest', by the way, only manifested as they partnered with God.

(c) See diagram over the page: Time to entry.

With this insight the action at Jericho makes complete sense. Normally, men of war would taunt the opposition to incite fear, like the intimidation used by Goliath on Saul's army (3). There was none of that at Jericho because this scene was not your normal siege scenario with one nation pitted against another. This is why the Commander of the Lord's army, indicated to Joshua that He was not there to take sides in the conflict, but that He was there to oversight God's judgment, as indicated by the drawn sword in His hand (4). This judgment was foretold in God's promise to Abram when He said, '*for the iniquity of the Amorites is not yet full*' (5).

It is also understandable that the only voice heard at Jericho apart from the final shout was the voice of the trumpets carrying the high praises of God. This was the Spirit of God's decrees against an unrepentant city.

The very Presence of the Commander of the Lord's host would suggest that there were angels with Him (6) who heard 637 years of charges being decreed by the voice of the trumpets. Thus, high praise was a '*two-edged sword*' that released the judgment of God, so that justice could be meted

(1) Malachi 4:2. (2) Hebrews 4:11. (3) 1 Samuel 17:10-11; 44 - 47 cf. Isaiah 36:12-20. (4) Joshua 5:13-14. (5) Genesis 15:16. (6) cf. Matthew 26:53.

out by Joshua and his men. This is just like a later incident when Jehoshaphat, under the direction of the voice of the Spirit (1), had singers go out before the army. The Bible says, that when the singers, *'began to sing and praise, the LORD set ambushes against...'* the enemy (2). Who was this unseen host ambushing the enemy? It was His angels, *'...who excel in strength, who do His word, heeding the voice of His word'* (3)!

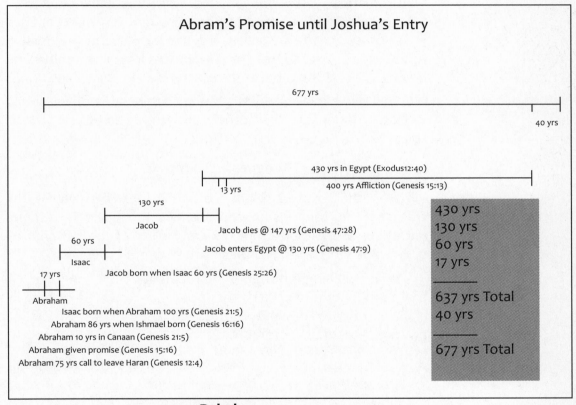

Abram's Promise until Joshua's Entry

677 yrs

40 yrs

430 yrs in Egypt (Exodus 12:40)

13 yrs

400 yrs Affliction (Genesis 15:13)

130 yrs

Jacob

Jacob dies @ 147 yrs (Genesis 47:28)

60 yrs

Jacob enters Egypt @ 130 yrs (Genesis 47:9)

Isaac

17 yrs

Jacob born when Isaac 60 yrs (Genesis 25:26)

Abraham

Isaac born when Abraham 100 yrs (Genesis 21:5)
Abraham 86 yrs when Ishmael born (Genesis 16:16)
Abraham 10 yrs in Canaan (Genesis 21:5)
Abraham given promise (Genesis 15:16)
Abraham 75 yrs call to leave Haran (Genesis 12:4)

430 yrs
130 yrs
60 yrs
17 yrs

637 yrs Total
40 yrs

677 yrs Total

(c) diagram: Time to entry

Rahab

Rahab, the prostitute, and her family were the only souls redeemed from the city. She was saved from judgment by

(1) 2 Chronicles 20:14. (2) 2 Chronicles 20:22. (3) Psalm 103:20; cf. Joel 2:11.

receiving two witnesses (1) and then hanging a scarlet thread from her window, representing the blood of Christ sprinkled on her heart (2). Does this suggest that the razing of Jericho prefigures the complete judgment upon sin meted out upon Christ at Calvary? Definitely! Just as Jericho was the gate into the Promised Land, so the cross of Christ is the path through which all must tread to enter the promises of God. Just as her walls of pride were removed, Jesus became ashamed for us (3). Just as God used Israel to enact judgment upon Jericho, He also used men to execute judgment on sin, in the Person of Christ (4). Just as everything within Jericho was devoted to destruction, so Jesus became accursed for us (5).

This also explains why Israel was to take none of the spoils of war; because this wasn't their fight, it was an offering made to the Lord.

Tongues as Trumpets

With the scriptural evidence of the interchangeability of trumpets and tongues in scripture, and these Old Testament narratives as examples, our understanding of the benefits of prayer and worship in tongues can't help but grow.

When we sing in tongues we recognize the connection of the ram's horn and Christ's sacrifice, and invoke the strength and authority of the Spirit of the Lord to usher in the blessing given to Abram our forefather;

'That in blessing I will bless you, and in multiplying I will multiply your seed as the stars of the heaven, and as the sand which is upon the sea shore; and your seed shall possess the gate of his enemies.'

Genesis 22:17 (KJV)

(1) Joshua 2:4, 9-11. (2) Joshua 2:18. (3) Matthew 27:27-30. (4) 2 Corinthians 5:21. (5) Galatians 3:13.

The latter part of this promise, of possessing '*the gate of his enemies*', was true of Joshua and his men in their use of shofars to see Jericho overthrown. It was true of Christ, as powerfully expressed in the Psalms, '*In the midst of the assembly I will praise You*' (1). In a Psalm recognized as portraying Christ upon the cross, Jesus is praising God in the midst of His ordeal, and from which position He rises with the gates of hell on His shoulders (2). It is equally true for us as God's children, that as we worship in tongues a two-edged sword is deployed in the Spirit, bringing praise to God on the one side, and judgment to God's enemies on the other. As the Psalmists again confirm,

> '*Let the saints be joyful in glory…. Let the high praises of God be in their mouth, and a two-edged sword in their hand; To execute vengeance upon the heathen, and punishments upon the people; To bind their kings with chains, and their nobles with fetters of iron; To execute upon them the judgment written: this honour have all his saints.*
>
> *Praise the Lord!*'

Psalm 149:5-9 (KJV)

As we sing in the Spirit (3), or as the Psalmist puts it, express the '*high praises of God*', our God fights for us (4) with His angels deployed to ambush the enemy and derail his plans. In this way our voices become '*the fountains of the great deep*' which initiate the opening of '*the windows of heaven*' and combine to bring judgment on the spiritual enemies of God (5). In addition, praying and singing in the Spirit brings us into His Rest (6) just as trumpets are used to usher in the Sabbath, New Year and Jubilee. We have been anointed (7) to proclaim in the Spirit,

> '*…the acceptable year of the LORD,*
> *And the day of vengeance of our God….*'

Isaiah 61:2

(1) Psalm 22:22. (2) Ephesians 5:19; Judges 16:3; Matthew 16:18; Isaiah 9:6. (3) 1 Corinthians 14:15. (4) Nehemiah 4:20. (5) Genesis 7:11. (6) Isaiah 28:11-12. (7) Isaiah 61:1.

This verse takes the shape of a two-edged sword that both rejoices in His perpetual Jubilee and, at the same time, releases judgment on the enemies of God (d).

(d) In the same way that a burnt offering produces both the rising of smoke in worship, and the destruction of the animal offered.

(e) Namaan dipped seven times bringing him into rest (2 Kings 5:14).

In this chapter, Joshua received a visitation that brought revelation. He was directed not to make accusations against the enemy, but rather, to take deliberate steps to release the voice of the Spirit of God through trumpets, which, with the aid of angelic intervention, brought God's judgment on Jericho.

It takes humility to rest (e). That doesn't mean you do nothing, it means you rest from your own labors and do what the Spirit directs you to do. Sometimes that may mean doing more than you would under the law. This is witnessed in Israel entering into 'rest' through the victory at Jericho. This was achieved when they gave themselves to be used of God beyond works (they broke the Sabbath), and in humility yielded their own tongues (1) which is the last vestige of human independence to God (2).

As we pray and sing in tongues, we, too, step into the 'rest' that sees the manifestation of the promises of God, humbly volunteering ourselves as vessels of praise, so that the Spirit of God may declare through us His unbiased favor and judgments.

(1) Isaiah 53:7b; cf. Psalm 12:4. (2) James 3:2-8.

Prayer:

Pray and sing in the Spirit today, knowing that as you do:

- God is releasing angels to both ambush the enemy and perform His word
- it is a two-edged sword in your mouth:
  - bringing high praises to God
  - meting out judgment on God's enemies.

Summary:

- A trumpet is a voice.
- Trumpets marked:
  - the gathering of the assembly
  - the journeying of the camps
  - preparation for war
  - a memorial before God
  - the beginning of the Sabbath
  - the year of Jubilee
  - God's promise to Abraham
  - entry into His 'rest'.
- Bringing heaven's purposes to earth takes more than obedience to a set of rules. Supernatural outbreaks of the power of God call for obedience beyond the law.
- The circumnavigation of Jericho by priests blowing trumpets represented the years of judgment pronounced against it.
- Angels worked with the high praises of God in the mouths of Joshua's trumpeting priests to bring judgment on Jericho.
- Singing in tongues, as connected to the ram's horn, releases the blessing of God pronounced over Abraham at the Akedah.
- Tongues releases a two-edged sword: praise to God on one side, and judgment on God's enemies on the other.
- Rest doesn't mean we do nothing, it means we rest from our own labors and do what the Spirit directs us to do.

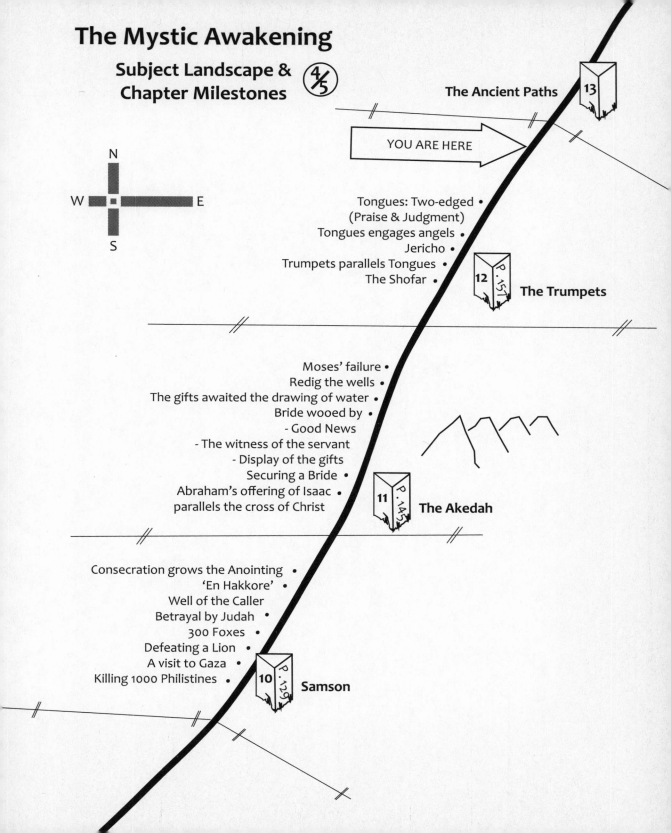

Chapter 13

The Ancient Paths

We have previously touched on the subject of the 'ancient paths' by focusing on 'the altar' as the place of entry and upon some men of renown who walked in the eternal realm. In this chapter I want to open what, I believe, is the map of the ancient paths that God has repeatedly provided throughout scripture.

The last day of Elijah's earthly life is a record of what seems like a series of random places he and Elisha visit on their way to his chariot-ride departure into heaven (1). In keeping with the mystic nature of the call, nothing is recorded of Elisha's training, instead his development is encoded in the sequence of events that unfold on that day. Each of the sites visited depict aspects of the journey, a journey that maps the ancient path into the eternal realms. A journey, therefore, that is truly more caught, than taught.

(1) 2 Kings 2:1-14.

Gilgal --> Bethel --> Jericho --> Jordan

Gilgal

In travelling from Gilgal, to Bethel, and then on to Jericho, before crossing the Jordan River, God has provided an outline of Elisha's apprenticeship. Gilgal means 'Circle', but is better defined by its use in scripture (a).

(a) A word dictionary may give a surface meaning. However, a better understanding of the meaning of words is often gained by observing their use in different passages of scripture.

Gilgal was the place where Joshua was instructed to circumcise the generation of men born in the wilderness, to replace those who were denied entry because of unbelief (1). On that occasion God said to Joshua, '*This day I have rolled away the reproach of Egypt from you*' (2). The word, '*reproach*' refers to a verbal taunt hurled by an enemy. The verse then continues, '*Therefore the name of the place is called Gilgal to this day*' (3). Gilgal is also the place where Joshua was instructed to place 12 stones from the midst of the Jordan as a memorial (a stone for each tribe). This was the place '*where the priests feet stood firm*' (4), when the waters of the Jordan were cut off before the ark (5).

To understand what Gilgal means in the context of Elisha's life, we must first consider its history and meaning to Israel. While it is legitimate to give the meaning of Gilgal either on its literal translation, 'Circle', or as, 'Rolling' (from a partial interpretation of God's word after the circumcision of Joshua's men), I believe another is warranted. The 12 gemstones on the breastplate of the High Priest represent the 12 tribes of Israel, so dear to the heart of God, so when we see the 12 river stones, which also represent the 12 tribes, picked from the Jordan we understand it symbolises the revealing or reemergence of the love of God for His people, Israel. It gives meaning to the reproach that was rolled away, which was referenced by Moses as part of his intercession for Israel's rebellion and their

(1) Numbers 14:11; Hebrews 4:11. (2) Joshua 5:9. (3) Joshua 5:9. (4) Joshua 4:3. (5) Joshua 4:2-3, 6-7, 20.

failure to enter the first time.

> *'Then the Egyptians will hear of it…then the nations which have heard of Your fame will speak saying, "Because the LORD was not able to bring this people to the land which He swore to give them, therefore He killed them in the wilderness."'*

Numbers 14:13, 15-16 (KJV Modernized)

The insults hurled at Israel because their God didn't have enough power to finish what He started, no longer apply, as He again demonstrates His power - in rolling back Jordan - and brings His people into that which was promised (1).

With that backdrop, the scene of Elisha journeying from Gilgal speaks of the lifting of a similar reproach from his life. When God called him through the throwing of the mantle of Elijah, he was in the despised position of plowing in the dust of eleven other plowmen who were ahead of him (2). When God told Elijah to anoint Elisha as his replacement (3) it meant that he was on God's heart, and that, should he take up the call, he would enter his destiny.

Bethel

Bethel means 'House of God'. When Elisha kissed his father and mother after he had received the call, he was signifying his departure from their household to be grafted into God's under the fatherhood of Elijah (4).

Jericho

We have seen that Jericho is the site of Israel's first 'victory' on entering Canaan, and that is the basic meaning given the city (5). It is also known as *'the City of Palms'* (6), which, similarly speaks of victory, as demonstrated when Jesus made His

---

(1) Joshua 3:15-17. (2) 1 Kings 19:19; cf. 2 Kings 2:23. (3) 1 Kings 19:16. (4) 1 Kings 19:20. (5) Joshua 6. (6) Deuteronomy 34:3; Judges 1:16; 3:13; 2 Chronicles 28:15.

triumphant entry and palms were thrown at His feet (1). For Elisha, this stage of the journey represents reaching maturity as a son.

Jordan

Jordan is such an important landmark within the journeying of Israel. It means, 'Death' or, 'Descender'. When the ark was carried across the Jordan, the waters rolled back to a town called '*Adam*', signifying that in Christ's death, sin and death rolled back to the first man, Adam (2). We, like Israel, may have entry through Christ's death into the promises of God, our Promised Land. For Elisha, Jordan signifies a willingness to lay down his life so that God would be given full expression through him.

Cover to Cover

If the journey of Gilgal through to Jordan is truly representative of the ancient paths, you would expect it to be found in the life of others who make the same pilgrimage in scripture. The truth is, that the path into the eternal realms in the journeys of its people is to be found from cover to cover of the Bible (See table on the following page).

Joseph

In the life of Jacob's son, Joseph, the journey is outlined in two ways. Firstly, in the outward circumstances he experiences, and then it is also documented in the progressive changes in his heart, as measured by what comes out of his mouth (3).

When Joseph was a young man his father, Jacob, gave him a coat of many colors. The coat was a prophetic sign that one day he would be great and would be clothed in glory (Gilgal) (4). He was then given a dream by God that not only confirmed he was called to lead (5), but that, of all Jacob's sons, God's

(1) Matthew 21:8. (2) Joshua 3:16; Romans 6:23. (3) Matthew 12:34b.
(4) Genesis 37:3. (5) Genesis 37:5

Elisha	Gilgal	Bethel	Jericho	Jordan
Patriarchs	Predestined	Called	Justified	Glorified
House		Wisdom	Understanding	Knowledge
Paul	Saul			Paul
Paul	Damascus	Brother	Wilderness	Filled Holy Spirit
Paul				That I may know Him
Paul		Hope	Faith	Love
Israel	Abraham (Gen.)	Lamb (Ex.)	Wilderness (Deut.)	Promised Land (Josh.)
Joseph	Coat	Dream	Prison	Prime Minister
Joseph		I	Belong to God	Not in me
Shulamite		Mine/His	His/Mine	His
John	Heir	Children	Sons	Fathers
Nicodemus		Born Again	Water	Spirit
John	John 13:3	John 14	John 15	John 17
John		House	Abide word	One
Abraham	Abram	Abraham		
Abraham	Haran	Bethel	Beersheba	Mt. Moriah
Overcomer		Blood	Word	Death
Overcomer	Rev. 17: 14	Called	Faithful	Chosen
Jesus		Way	Truth	Life
Jesus		LOE	LOF	POL
Seed		30	60	100
Way *	Eagle	Snake	Ship	Woman
Psalm 1		Walk	Stand	Sit
David	Anointed	Saul's Minstrel	Wilderness	King
Tabernacle		Outer Court	Holy Place	Holy of Holies
River**	Ankles	Knees	Waist	Out of our depth

Table b: The Ancient Paths throughout Scripture.

LOE: Lust of the eyes; LOF: Lust of the flesh; POL: Pride of Life.
See note (f) in this chapter.
* Proverbs 30: 18-19.
** Ezekiel 47:2-5.

promise to the household of Abraham would be fulfilled through him (Bethel). These projections of his future saw him sold into slavery by his brothers (Jericho), which ended with him being thrown in prison. He eventually came out of prison (Jordan) and became Pharaoh's prime minister according to that which was predestined for him. Though Joseph had no control over the first two phases of his path into the glory, his role in the latter stages to fulfil his destiny was critical.

What Joseph said as he interpreted dreams along the way, progressively revealed his state of heart and the change he was undergoing. When he first had a dream, he said, '...*this dream which I have dreamed*', (1). At the next recorded opportunity to interpret he said, '*Do not interpretations belong to God? Tell them to me please,*' (2). And, finally, before Pharaoh, he said, '*It is not in me; God will give Pharaoh an answer of peace,*' (3). There was a continual change of heart which kept pace with his journey. At the outset Joseph was full of himself. In prison he puts God in the equation, but still includes himself, '*Do not interpretations belong to God? Tell them to me please,*'. This request by Joseph led to the interpretation of the dreams of a 'bread'-maker, who was 'broken', and a 'wine'-bearer who was 'resurrected'. I believe this brought him to his own personal death and resurrection experience (Jordan) (b). When he came before Pharaoh there was none of the old Joseph present; he was a totally surrendered vessel through which God's glory could manifest. He says, '*It is not in me; God will give Pharaoh an answer of peace*'.

(b) The bread was broken (death) while the wine was lifted (resurrected).

Predestined, Called, Justified and Glorified

The journey is seen in the cumulative story of the Patriarchs, Abraham, Isaac, Jacob and Joseph, who together, are the reference for Paul's encouragement to the Roman church,

(1) Genesis 37:6. (2) Genesis 40:8. (3) Genesis 41:16.

'Moreover whom he did <u>predestinate</u>, them he also <u>called</u>:
and whom he called, them he also <u>justified</u>:
and whom he justified, them he also <u>glorified</u>.'

Romans 8:30 (KJV, Emphasis added)

Gilgal aligns with being predestined to move into the Promised Land, as the place of the revealing of the heart of God (1); Bethel aligns with being *'called'*, in that the naming process is a mark of coming into the household of God (2); Jericho aligns with being *'justified'*, not by observance of the law, but rather, by being right with God by faith in His word (3); and Jordan aligns with being *'glorified'*, as the place of passing through death into a resurrection of the fullness of the Spirit (4).

When Paul penned these words to the Roman church, he applied them to those, *'who love God, to those called according to His purpose'* (5), and sealed the beneficiaries of such a blessing, by saying,

'He who did not spare His own Son, but delivered Him up for us all, how shall He not with Him also freely give us all things?'

Romans 8:32

In doing so, he accounted that pronouncement of predestination into glory to all believers. This means that we are all somewhere on the path, but that though it is freely given, not everyone is aware of the map before them.

Wisdom, Understanding and Knowledge

In the Book of Proverbs the ancient path is described in terms of wisdom, understanding and knowledge and is perhaps best captured by the verse that reads,

'Through <u>wisdom</u> a house is built

---

(1) Genesis 11:31; 12:1. (2) Genesis 17:19; Hebrews 11:18. (3) Genesis 48:3-4, 15-16; Hebrews 11:21. (4) Genesis 41:38-43. (5) Romans 8:28.

> *And by <u>understanding</u> it is established;*
> *By <u>knowledge</u> the rooms are filled*
> *With all precious and pleasant riches.'*

Proverbs 24:3-4 (Emphasis added)

Couched in poetic terms this passage documents the journey from Bethel to Jordan. In keeping with its poetic nature this is not the world's wisdom, understanding or knowledge, but must be viewed from a heavenly perspective. In the world one accrues knowledge and is considered wise; in the economy of God, wisdom is the door into the eternal realm where one has access to the mind of Christ (1) (c). Wisdom speaks of revelation of the reality of our spirit man, which is enclosed in the house (2); understanding relates to obedience to that which is received by faith, whereby our spirits become strengthened (d), and knowledge is that which steps across the veil beyond human knowledge into an experiential knowledge of God (3).

(c) The mind of Christ is God's revelation to the heart on a matter.

(d) Faith is linked to understanding the word. Faith's 'under'standing is obedience to the rhema word.

cf. Hebrews 11:3. *'Through faith we understand'*.

Song of Songs

Similar to the inward journey undertaken by Joseph, the Song of Songs documents the progression between Bethel and Jordan in terms captured by the Shulamite's love,

'My beloved is mine, and I am his....'

Song of Songs 2:16

'I am my beloved's and my beloved is mine.'

Song of Songs 6:3

'I am my beloved's, and his desire is toward me.'

Song of Songs 7:10

(1) 1 Corinthians 2:16. (2) 2 Corinthians 5:1. (3) Ephesians 3:19.

Although the first two expressions of love both express reciprocal love, they are very different. In the first, the primary need is on getting, '*My beloved is mine,*' before a reciprocal measure is returned to her lover, '*and I am his*'. In the second, this order has been turned around, so that now the emphasis is first on giving, '*I am my beloved's*' which precedes a continuing need for security, '*and my beloved is mine*'. However, the development of love in the first two stages is eclipsed by the last expression, where there is a total abandonment into the love of her lover. She is now secure in his love and is so certain of his heart toward her that she has lost all awareness of 'self'. She now exists in him.

Bethel speaks of a childhood love that needs constant assurance, Jericho sees a maturing take place as, 'He' becomes the adoring focus, before passing through Jordan where there is a realization of the depth of His love.

Israel

For the nation of Israel, the journey is seen in the exodus from Egypt and culminates in entry to the Promised Land. God's plan to bring Israel out of Egypt existed long before Moses encountered the burning bush (Gilgal) (1). God brought them out marked by the death of the Passover lamb for a household (Bethel) (2). Then, after passing through the Red Sea, they entered the wilderness where they learnt that,

'*...man shall not live by bread alone;*
but man lives by every word that proceeds from the mouth of
the LORD.'

Deuteronomy 8:3

Israel's sojourn in the wilderness imparted the principle of living by faith, that they, on hearing His voice, would be able to

(1) Genesis 15:13-14. (2) Exodus 12:3.

move in and take possession of what was promised (Jericho). Their failure to realize this last step saw them delayed in crossing the River Jordan, until a new generation stepped into the destiny by leaving the past behind and crossing over into the Promised Land (Jordan).

The Book of Revelation

'And they overcame him by <u>the blood</u> of the Lamb
and by <u>the word</u> of their testimony,
and they did <u>not love their lives</u> to the death.'

Revelation 12:11 (Emphasis added)

How important is it that we recognize this path and get on it? This verse says it is critical to overcoming the accuser of the brethren, the devil (1). Do you mean we will be oppressed by the enemy and tossed to and fro playing church until we wake up and get back on track? I'm not saying that, the Bible is!

Hopefully by now you can see the path in the above verse. This verse is a declaration in heaven that maps the eternal path from Bethel to Jordan. The purchase price of the blood of the Lamb has translated us legally out of satan's household into the Son's (2) (Bethel). The *'word of their testimony'* is not the record of their conversion, as some interpret this passage. The *'word of their testimony'* is the 'rhema' (spoken or living word of God), received, in our mouth, and acted upon. This is the substance of faith that brings forth victorious manifestation (Jericho). The last part of the verse is not an emphasis on martyrdom, but rather, an enveloping in love (Jordan). The essence of this part of the verse is caught in Song of Songs, where it is stated, *'For love is as strong as death'* (3). The various angles provided by each of the above examples help us better interpret this verse as a whole. As we saw in the progression of

(1) Revelation 12:10. (2) 1 Corinthians 6:19. (3) Song of Songs 8:6.

the Shunamite's love, this final step depicts being so caught up in the ecstasy of His love, that 'self' is dead.

Paul

Some may be questioning the applicability of this path today. After all, didn't Jesus say *'it is finished!'*? And there is a measure of confusion being caused by those who say that Paul's teachings on grace supplant that which came earlier. So, are we re-entering works by embracing the ancient path?

What if the ancient path were evident in Paul's life? The Apostle Paul didn't start out being named Paul. He was formerly known as Saul and, as Saul, he persecuted the church until one day on the road to Damascus he encountered Christ (1). This was not a chance meeting. Jesus told Ananias, the disciple He sent to welcome him into the family, *'Go, for he is a chosen vessel of Mine to bear My name before Gentiles...'* (2). This indicates that God had predestined Saul to become Paul (Gilgal). Saul was referred to by Ananias as *'Brother Saul...'* (3), which denotes him as a member of the household of faith in Jesus Christ (Bethel). After a brief interlude in Jerusalem Saul was sent to Tarsus where he was unheard of for a period of time until Barnabas went seeking him (4) (Jericho). He worked under the leadership of Barnabas in Antioch for more than a year until he was sent (again, under Barnabas' leadership) on a mission trip to Cyprus and the isle of Paphos (5). It is here, in Paphos and confronted by Elymas the sorcerer, that Saul, filled with the Holy Spirit, is officially recognized as Paul (Jordan) (6). *'Saul'* means, 'asked for' or 'demanded', whereas *'Paul'* means 'Little, humble'. Clearly, Saul's journey from the Damascus Road to the Isle of Paphos not only follows the Gilgal to Jordan route that has been outlined, but, like Joseph, has an internal journey which is also documented in his name change (e). Further to this, his progress is signposted, in terms of the path in Proverbs

(e) Saul (demanded) to Paul (little/humble).

Does Paul embrace greater meekness in His presence?

55AD *'least of the apostles'* (1 Corinthinians 15:9)

61 AD *'less than the least'* (Ephesians 3:8)

63-66AD *'chief of sinners'* (1 Timothy 1:15)

(1) Acts 9:1, 3-5. (2) Acts 9:15. (3) Acts 9:17. (4) Acts 9:28, 30; 11:25. (5) Acts 11:26; 13:4, 6. (6) Acts 13:9.

(wisdom, understanding, knowledge), by his words to the Philippian church. He says,

> *'That I may <u>know Him</u>, and the power of His resurrection,*
> *and the fellowship of His sufferings,*
> *being conformed to His death.'*

> Philippians 3:10 (Emphasis added)

So the man who is credited with unfolding grace to the church walked this ancient path. Selah. This is because the 'ancient paths' are timeless (Hebrew: Ancient = Olam = Eternal). That is, they do not change. The route that applied before the cross also applies after the cross, because it is eternal (outside of time).

Hope, Faith and Love

Not only did Paul walk the ancient path, he indirectly taught it as well, notably when he penned the words, *'and now abide, faith, hope, love...but the greatest of these is love,'* (1). Making reference to whatever 'abides' or 'remains' is a declaration that these three cardinal virtues are eternal. It is no coincidence that when arranged as hope, faith and love they align exactly with the locations of Bethel to Jordan in what we are calling the ancient or eternal path.

(f) Path of Jesus' temptation: lust of the flesh (stones to bread) overcome by *faith*, pride of life (throw yourself down) overcome by *love*, lust of the eyes (all these things) overcome by *hope*. Matthew 4:1-11.

On a geographic map of Israel, Elijah and Elisha's journey from Gilgal to Jordan does not run on a straight line. It comes as no surprise, then, that as the occasion demands there are variations to the path. Similarly, the record of Jesus' three-phased temptation in the wilderness (f) is recorded in a different order in Matthew's and Luke's accounts so this living and dynamic path is not to be merely followed as a formula (2).

Hope, which aligns with coming into the House of God (Bethel), speaks of the promise of life ahead for those who,

(1) 1 Corinthians 13:13. (2) Matthew 4:1-11; Luke 4:1-13.

by faith, are prepared to apprehend it. That all do not avail themselves to see the promise manifest is attested to by Jesus' words, '*For many are called, but few chosen*' (1). The word, '*chosen*' is reference to reaching a certain benchmark which, Christ Himself acknowledged, was the goal.

The Bible teaches that faith comes by hearing the rhema word of God (2), and that faith is our victory (3). Therefore, the association between 'Faith' and 'Jericho' is pretty straightforward. Israel came to victory at Jericho by being obedient to the rhema of instruction from the Commander of the Lord's army.

Indeed, love is the greatest, because it is the goal Christ had in mind for all believers. Love is not merely what God does, it is who He is, for '*God is love*' (4). Therefore, when we love He is expressing Himself through us. Love is the motivation and disposition to experience heaven on earth.

The Apostle Paul, the cardinal virtues and the ancient path are inextricably linked when Paul lifts the vision above any debate about grace and works and endorses the ancient path to define the '*new creation*'. He says,

> '*For in Christ Jesus neither circumcision*
> *nor uncircumcision avails anything,*
> *but <u>faith</u> working through <u>love</u>.*'

> Galatians 5:6 (Emphasis added)

And again,

> '*For in Christ Jesus neither circumcision*
> *nor uncircumcision avails anything,*
> *but <u>a new creation</u>.*'

> Galatians 6:15 (Emphasis added)

(1) Matthew 20:16; 22:14. (2) Romans 10:17. (3) 1 John 5:4. (4) 1 John 4:8.

Hence, the new creation is faith working through love. Here we have the dynamic nature of the journey confirmed. Having embraced love, a person doesn't move on from faith, but partners faith and love to see new creation realities manifest.

Children, Sons and Fathers

John the Apostle, himself a mystic, makes reference to the ancient path on more than one occasion. I draw your attention to three verses in his first letter where he uses poetic construction to outline another perspective of the ancient path.

> '*I write to you, little <u>children</u>,*
> *Because your sins are forgiven you for His name's sake.*
> *I write to you, <u>fathers</u>,*
> *Because you have known Him who is from the beginning.*
> *I write to you, <u>young men</u>,*
> *Because you have overcome the wicked one.*
> *I write to you, little <u>children</u>,*
> *Because you have known the Father.*
> *I have written to you, <u>fathers</u>*
> *Because you have known Him who is from the beginning.*
> *I have written to you, <u>young men</u>,*
> *Because you are strong, and the word of God abides in you,*
> *And you have overcome the wicked one.*'

1 John 2:12-14 (Emphasis added)

These verses document the spiritual path to maturity. The progression is anchored against a metaphor from everyday Jewish life: that of commencing as children, growing into sons (young men), and then maturing to become fathers. These landmarks of maturity parallel the sequence of locations on Elijah and Elisha's journey. A person at Bethel is a child of God, who has had his sins forgiven and has known the Father (1).

(1) cf. 1 John 3:1.

Sons, on the other hand, are those at Jericho, who are strong, having the word of God abiding in them, and, as a consequence, have overcome the wicked one. Fathers are those at Jordan, who have come to know Him who is from the beginning.

That this path is relevant and applicable to us is seen in the fact that John's starting point - children - is the born-again experience of having our sins forgiven. It is inconceivable that once on this path, God would not want us to grow up! The Scriptures tell us that He does not want us to, '*remain as children, tossed to and fro with every wind of doctrine...*' (1). He wants us to mature by undertaking the journey. That is outlined by '*abiding in the word*', which speaks of more than accumulating head knowledge of Scripture. It refers to becoming attuned to receive the 'rhema' or spoken word, so that it may find expression living in and through us. It is this word that overcomes the enemy. According to the opening verse of John's first letter, He who is from the beginning is Christ (2), and we know from our earlier discussion on knowledge (in Proverbs) that this refers to an experiential and not intellectual knowledge. Therefore, a true father is not merely someone in church leadership, but a person who has learned to walk as one with Christ, and as such, is an extension of Him as a father, freely dispensing facets of His love and truth. Little wonder that the Apostle Paul wrote to the Corinthian church saying, '*For though you have ten thousand instructors in Christ, yet you have not many fathers...*' (3).

Jesus said '*whoever offends one of these little ones...*'. Matthew 18:6. Therefore those that are offended are children.

John's Gospel

John's gospel is more than a historic record of Jesus' life, it is deliberately mystical in design and content. The book of John has been divided into 21 chapters, which span Christ's three and half years of ministry. In the middle of the Book are five chapters dedicated to Christ's farewell discourse with His disciples which took place over a few hours (4). The fact that so much space - a

(1) Ephesians 4:14 (2) 1 John 1:1. (3) 1 Corinthians 4:15. (4) John 13-17.

quarter of the Book - has been allocated to such a relatively short time span tells us that the content of that discussion is critically important. A very brief overview of Jesus' parting words reveals that we are to be God's house (1) (g); that His disciples are to abide in Him, and have His word abide in them (2); that the Holy Spirit was about to come (3), and that we are to become one with Him, just as He was one with the Father (4). I think it is conclusive that what Jesus imparted, at that critical hour, was modelled on the ancient path (h). Absolutely amazing! How important is it? After salvation and the new birth, an understanding of the ancient path is essential for spiritual growth.

The Way, Truth and the Life

In the midst of John's record of Jesus' farewell discourse he writes, *'I am the way, the truth, and the life...'* (5). Whilst there are several levels on which this verse can be interpreted, once you are alerted to see the ancient paths it virtually jumps off the page at you. *'The way'* is that which is opened through the blood of Christ, *'the truth'* is the rhema word (6), and *'the life'* is the Spirit of God.

This verse is packed with revelation, but two things stand out from the rest. The first is that the ancient path is not a formula, it is a person; the Person of the Lord Jesus Christ. And, secondly, Jesus, as *'the way, the truth, and the life'*, is not an all-in-one holiday destination, where you don't have to do a thing, but is more the lifelong travelling companion who is guiding you on a journey of discovery through heaven.

(g) John 14:2 'In My Father's house are many mansions' is not merely about a house in heaven, but a reality here on earth as well, as Jesus prepared a place in our hearts by dying on the cross to cleanse us. See note (a) chapter 3 'Jesus' mission'.

(h) In John's gospel the house of chapter 14, the word of chapter 15 and the union of chapter 17 equates to Bethel, Jericho, Jordan.

(1) John 14:2. (2) John 15:4, 7. (3) John 16:7. (4) John 17:21-23. (5) John 14:6. (6) John 17:17.

Prayer:

Father, I thank you that You have lifted me onto the Ancient Paths and have provided a 'map' throughout Scripture to guide me. I thank You that just as the great men and women of faith matured by traversing its trail I too have been given opportunity to follow the milestones that show the way. Therefore, teach me the progressive connection between hope, faith and love so that I will grow to be like Christ and see Your glory manifest in my life. Amen.

Summary:

- Elijah's last journey with Elisha maps the ancient paths.

- The journey: Gilgal>Bethel>Jericho> Jordan outlines Elisha's apprenticeship into the ancient paths.

- The ancient paths are found and delineated from cover to cover of the Bible.

- The journey taken by Joseph, Jacob's son, shows that the ancient path is as much an inward journey as it is an outward experience.

- The ancient paths are outlined in Paul's encouragement to lovers of God, as in, whom He predestines, He calls, He justifies and glorifies.

- The poetic books describe the ancient paths in terms of wisdom, understanding and knowledge.

- Song of Songs delineates the journey in terms of the growth of love within the Shulamite.

- In the Book of Revelation, John outlines the path in the progression of overcomers: through the Blood, the word of their testimony and loving not their own lives unto death.

- Paul, the apostle, who expounded grace, models the ancient paths:

    - in his name change
    - in telling us that only faith, hope and love remain
    - in his cry to know Him
    - in his ever-increasing humility.

- John draws on a metaphor from Jewish life to outline the path as growing from being children, to young men, to fathers.

- His gospel also reveals the ancient paths in Jesus' final address to the twelve and in His declaration that He is the Way, Truth and the Life.

- The ancient path is not a formula, but a person: Jesus Christ.

Chapter 14

The Mystic Journey

Elisha's Apprenticeship

Like David before him, Elisha received an anointing, the promise of greater things, but, also like David, he had a journey to be traversed before he could step into the fullness of what was promised. Many people view their Christianity as a waiting game, a 'treading water' type experience, and are mistakenly awaiting death to enter heaven. Embracing the timeless ancient paths presents another point of view, one where salvation is the beginning of a journey beyond this world. It is a voyage of discovery, as it were, that begins the day you are born again. Christ is the navigational chart on the table before you, but you are the one unrolling it. This is a journey we clearly need a greater appreciation of, for it is the course we all need to travel to enter the eternal realms.

The Path to Spiritual Maturity
2 Kings 2:1-18

Elijah and Elisha took a path from Gilgal, through Bethel and Jericho, and then on to Jordan. This was a journey to spiritual maturity, from a place of recognition that there was an inheritance to be gained (Gilgal), and that led all the way to fatherhood (Jordan). It was also a journey of development in the eternal virtues of hope, faith and love, and one of ever-increasing personal surrender.

The Tests of the Journey

Three times during the trek Elijah suggested Elisha stay on at a location while he proceeded alone (1), and the sons of the prophets came twice to Elisha informing him of Elijah's impending departure (2). What are we to make of these incidents? Clearly they are indicative of the tests that present themselves along the way and Elisha's responses reveal the heart attitude that ensures graduation. In sequence these tests look like this,

Gilgal

- Elijah requests he stay here

Bethel

- Sons of the prophets voice their concern
- Elijah requests he stay here

Jericho

- Sons of the prophets voice their concern
- Elijah requests he stay here

At all three places Elijah said to Elisha, '*Stay here, please, for the LORD has sent me on...*' (3). Each time Elisha responded, '*As the Lord lives, and as your soul lives, I will not leave you!*' While

(1) 2 Kings 2:2, 4, 6. (2) 2 Kings 2:3, 5. (3) 2 Kings 2:2, 4, 6.

Elisha's response can genuinely be interpreted as, 'I swear I won't leave you', there is more to be found in the lives of both of these men that reveal what was behind Elisha's determination. Earlier in his ministry Elijah was quoted more than once, as saying, 'As the Lord God of Israel lives, before whom I stand...' (1). While this is a call for God to witness the truth of his words, it is also a declaration of his access to the Eternal One who has life in Himself. And it was this, I believe, that Elisha was determinedly after. He was successful in his quest because subsequent to Elijah's departure Elisha was also found using the same preface to his words (2). This is the *'life'* that Jesus referred to when He said, '*I am the way, the truth, and the LIFE*' (3), and this is the very tangible Presence available today.

This begs the question, 'If Elijah were a type of Christ, and Elisha a figure of us, would Christ be found going forward into the Father's presence, and asking us to stay where we are?' Surely not! Well, what if Elijah's request to stay at Gilgal, Bethel and Jericho were paralleled in Christ's ministry with His disciples?

Developing Spiritual Hope

When Elisha received his initial calling by the throwing of Elijah's mantle, Elijah followed it up by saying, '*Go back again, for what have I done to you?*' (4). In John's Gospel, Jesus said, '*My sheep hear My voice...and they follow Me*,' (5). Elisha evidently heard the word to follow, even though it was unspoken (6). In Elijah's command to return are Christ's words to '*count the cost*' (7) before you start out. At this early stage it is 'Hope' that carries Elisha onward to Bethel.

Bethel is the place of childhood hope, it is the place of potential; everything is there, but not yet unpacked. Elijah's request for his disciple to stay at Bethel was echoed in Jesus' words,

(1) 1 Kings 17:1; 18:15. (2) 2 Kings 3:14; 5:16. (3) John 14:6. (4) 1 Kings 19:20. (5) John 10:27. (6) 1 Kings 19:19. (7) Luke 14:28.

> *'He who loves father or mother more than Me*
> *is not worthy of Me.*
> *And he who loves son or daughter more than Me*
> *is not worthy of Me.'*

Matthew 10:37 (cf. Luke 14:26)

This is a controversial passage to interpret because it is so challenging to much we hold dear. However, it is evident that Elisha gave up his parents for the call (1). It is also plain from Elisha's example that the House of God (Bethel), is not the institutional church. This is not about abandoning your family for a denomination. On one level, this is a recognition that the blood of Jesus has brought you into the household of God, you now have His DNA running through your veins, and you are a totally new creation (2). You are no longer a mere member of the human race (3), God now is your Father (4), and He has called you to the family business of bringing the kingdom to earth (5). Compared to your previous closest relationships Jesus is now closer than a brother (6). His relationship with you supersedes all you have known before and is to take precedence in your life. What He says about you, is truth; you are no longer to wear what the world says about you.

On another level, you are no longer an earthly facade. You are now a brand new building site with its foundations prepared to receive precious stones from heaven. Your earthly parents were merely surrogates who brought you to this point of time. That is not to say you are to abdicate family responsibilities; in fact, with Christ in your life, you are the ambassador of Christ to your family. You are His representative and, as such, you will genuinely love them more (7).

If that offends you, you have stopped at Bethel. How strongly do you want to carry the Presence of the Living God? If we stay at the place of 'Hope' and do not see the promise

(1) 1 Kings 19:20. (2) 2 Corinthians 5:17. (3) John 1:12-13. (4) cf. Luke 2:49. (5) Matthew 6:10. (6) Proverbs 18:24. (7) 1 Peter 3:1-5.

materialize, we become disillusioned (1). Disillusioned saints become disinterested, and disinterested people become disengaged. It is 'Faith' that carries Elisha onward toward Jericho.

Developing Faith

Jericho speaks of living by faith as a son in the place of victory (2). At times Jesus said some pretty heavy things. One day He said to His disciples that they had to eat His flesh and drink His blood, which offended many of them and they ceased to follow Him (3). On seeing them leave, He didn't rally the troops and tell them to hunker down and that they would get through this. No, He said to them, *'Do you also want to go away?'* (4). Peter gave expression to what kept the twelve from leaving, when he proclaimed, *'Lord, to whom shall we go? You have the words of eternal life'* (5). What kept them was recognition that what He said came from the throne of God, engendering faith in them.

Living by faith calls for an obedience to the word received (a), and on many occasions requires stepping out beyond convention. God told Elijah to go to the Brook Cherith where he would be fed by ravens (6). In a religious culture which deemed ravens as an abomination that was a pretty radical instruction (7). Namaan, the leper, was told to go and wash in a dirty river so that he would be made clean (8). Now that defied logic. If directed by the Lord, how do you think you and I would feel about receiving financial assistance from a waitress in a topless bar, instruction from a practising homosexual, or healing prayer from the world's most-tattooed man? More than likely we would feel uncomfortable. Do we want to stop at Jericho? Again, let's remind ourselves how much we want what Jesus had, and press forward to carry the Presence of God.

(a) To hear means to obey.

Hear: sama (H8085): A verb meaning to hear, to obey, to listen, to be heard of, to be regarded, to cause to hear, to proclaim, to sound aloud. e.g. Deuteronomy 6:4.

(1) Proverbs 13:12; Psalm 27:13. (2) 1 John 5:4. (3) John 6:53-66. (4) John 6:67. (5) John 6:68. (6) 1 Kings 17:3-4. (7) Leviticus 11:13-15. (8) 2 Kings 5:10-12.

Dividing the Waters

The journey to Jordan is that which distinguishes fathers from sons, it is a crossing made by those who carry a love, '*as strong as death*' (1), and it was this that constrained Elisha to move onward (2).

When Elijah and Elisha departed from Jericho, the Bible records that they became distinguished from the other followers of God who remained at Jericho,

'*And fifty men of the sons of the prophets went, and stood to view afar off: and they two stood by Jordan.*'

2 Kings 2:7 (KJV)

I believe it is this distinction that is spiritually painted for us when, subsequently, they crossed over the Jordan. The scripture states,

'*And Elijah took his mantle, and wrapped it together, and smote the waters, and they were divided <u>hither</u> and <u>thither</u>, so that they two went over on dry ground.*'

2 Kings 2:8 (KJV, Emphasis added)

(b) Them: hennah (H2007)

feminine plural meaning 'they', 'them'.

I have deliberately used the KJV here because of its use of the words, 'hither' and, 'thither', which means 'them' and 'them'(b). What this is saying, is that there are two types of water, 'them' and 'them'. Water is that which we carry in our hearts, as in, a husband is to wash his wife in the water of the word (3), and '*...out of his heart will flow rivers of living water*' (4), and, '*Deep calls to deep*' (5). What this river crossing depicts, is the parting of the heart and words of men, from the heart and words of God. This distinction is manifest by the revelation of the parting of soul and Spirit seen in the striking of the water (6). And it is this distinction that opens the eternal realm of

(1) Song of Songs 8:6. (2) cf. 2 Corinthians 5:13. (3) Ephesians 5:26 .
(4) John 7:38. (5) Psalm 42:7. (6) 2 Kings 2:8; Hebrews 4:12; cf. John 6:63.

heaven and makes a path beyond the veil of death into His Presence. What does this look like? It looks like, loving others as yourself (c) to the point of self denial (death), and through such an act, access is gained into heaven so that, reciprocally, heaven manifests on earth. This is an example of, '...*If we love one another, God abides in us...*' (1).

Does Jesus expect such a level of commitment from us? It is clear that He does.

> '*If anyone comes to Me and does not hate...*
> *yes, and his own life, he cannot be My disciple.*'
>
> Luke 14:26

And,

> '*So therefore any one of you who does not renounce*
> *all that he has cannot be My disciple.*'
>
> Luke 14:33 (KJV Modernized)

Consider what Jesus said to the rich young ruler (2), or, on a more personal level, what the Apostle John wrote, which is closer to our hearts.

> '*But whoever has this world's goods,*
> *and sees his brother in need,*
> *and shuts up his heart from him,*
> *how does the love of God abide in him?*'
>
> 1 John 3:17

Each stage of the journey requires greater surrender, progressively more of Him and less of us (3). It comes down to how much we desire to carry the Presence. If you have read this far, chances are, like Peter, you have tasted something of heaven; you are forever spoiled for the ordinary, and compelled

(c) Loving others as yourself does not mean loving yourself first. By comparing Matthew 7:12 and Matthew 22:39-40 and knowing that the Law and the Prophets is reference to the Old Testament. Jesus is equating loving your neighbour as yourself with doing to others what you would have them do to you. Therefore, we discover the expression '*loving your neighbour as yourself*' means doing unto others what you yourself would want done to you.

---

(1) 1 John 4:12. (2) Mathew 19:16-22. (3) John 3:30.

to proclaim, *'Lord, to whom shall we go? You have the words of eternal life!'* (1). You know that nothing else satisfies.

Silencing the Voices of Unbelief

Now that we have trekked the route identifying the meaning of each location, what of the sons of the prophets who interject with the assertion that Elijah is leaving (2)? A strong indicator of what is going on here is conveyed by Elisha's response to them. At both Bethel and Jericho, Elisha shuts them down by saying, 'Be quiet!' However, Elisha's responses to their respective concerns address different issues at each location.

At Bethel, the place of childhood 'Hope', he silenced the voice of dependence on the 'seen' realm. The sons of the prophets at Bethel who have not yet graduated to Jericho, the place where 'Sons grow in Faith', still have a propensity to live by what they see. Elijah's departure threatened their dependence on seeing him in order to receive from God. They were learning to receive prophetic downloads, but were still prone to be swayed by the outward world, or the desire of the eyes (3). In other words, the sons of the prophets at Bethel are a picture of those learning to distinguish between earthly and heavenly hope.

'For we were saved in this hope,
but hope that is seen is not hope:
for why does one still hope for what he sees.'

Romans 8:24

This is in accordance with the opening verse of the faith chapter in the Book of Hebrews, which states,

(1) John 6:67. (2) 2 Kings 2:3, 5. (3) 1 John 2:16.

*'Now faith is the substance of things hoped for,
the evidence of things not seen.'*

Hebrews 11:1

At Jericho, when Elisha again shut down the sons of the prophets, he did so with a different rationale. At Jericho, he is now at the place of 'Sons growing in Faith', he is silencing the voice of 'reason' that would seek to limit him to their perception of him as Elijah's servant. That's a voice that does not consider the spiritual dimension, but has a ceiling based on earthly experience and logic (d). When Abraham's faith was similarly challenged by physical restriction - his age - the scriptures record,

(d) Be aware that our thoughts are often formed around our emotions.

> *'And being not weak in faith, he considered not his own body now dead, when he was about a hundred years old, neither yet the deadness of Sarah's womb: He staggered not at the promise of God through unbelief; but was strong in faith, giving glory to God.'*

Romans 4:19-20 (KJV)

Elisha was closing down an opportunity for the unbelief of others to rob him of the promise attached to his apprenticeship. This unbelief was based on their need for Elijah, their hero of faith, to be physically present. What is on display here is a dependence on the material world, in contrast to the spirit one (1). Like Jesus' disciples, the sons of the prophets could not see the advantage in him going away (2). This dependence was displayed by fifty of their number who, even knowing prophetically of Elijah's departure (3), insisted in searching for him when Elisha returned from the Jordan without him (4). Though growing in faith, their propensity to be restricted by physical limitations also explains why they stood afar off as Elijah and Elisha went on alone to cross the boundary of Jordan

(1) 1 John 2:16. (2) John 16:7. (3) 2 Kings 2:5. (4) 2 Kings 2:16-18.

into the eternal realm (1). It should be noted that once they had seen one man break through the mental limitation they were under, they too were able to move on to dwell at Jordan (2).

The Double Portion

When Elijah and Elisha had gone over the Jordan, Elijah requested that his intern ask what he desired from him before he was taken from him (3). This is a reminder that prayer enters the eternal realm beyond the veil of the material world and sees results that are impossible to man but possible for God (4). Like us, Elisha was given right of entry by the death (crossing Jordan) of his master.

What Elisha asks is for '*a double portion*' of Elijah's spirit (5). Elisha performed twice as many miracles as Elijah, which on one level could confirm that he received what he asked for. However, his request suggests he wanted not an earthly motivated literal 'double' of what Elijah had (e), but the double portion due to the firstborn son (6). This is a request for the blessing to be bestowed from father to eldest son. He desired Divine equipping to now move into the fatherhood role that was being vacated by Elijah (7). His was not the request of an immature prodigal son, but the concern of a would-be-father who would now take up the tutorage of the sons of the prophets. May I suggest, in recognizing Elijah as a prequel to Christ, that Elisha performed twice the works of Elijah because God is reminding us of the '*greater*' works that await us (8).

An interesting side story is that although Elijah was commanded to anoint three men (9), he only anointed one of them, namely, Elisha. However, Elisha, some ten years later, anointed the other two (10). This suggests Elijah was in Elisha doing the works, just as Christ is in us. Selah.

(e) That is inconceivable, seeing he has overcome the lust of the eyes (seen realm) through the blood at Bethel; has overcome the material limitations and impossibility of Jericho, by faith, as the word of his testimony; to now, go through Jordan, which represents the death of his independency or pride (Revelation 12:11; 1 John 2:15-16).

(1) 2 Kings 2:7. (2) 2 Kings 6:1-2. (3) 2 Kings 2:9. (4) Matthew 19:26. (5) 2 Kings 2:9. (6) Deuteronomy 21:17. (7) cf. Genesis 48:14-20. (8) John 14:12. (9) 1 Kings 19:15-16. (10) 2 Kings 8:13; 9:1-3.

A Hard Thing

The bottom line for mystics, is the passing over of the mantle, which presents the importance of the relationship between our surrender and seeing in the Spirit. The interaction recorded between the two men leads us into the climatic scene. Elisha asked for, '*a double portion*', and Elijah responded, '*You have asked a hard thing*' (1). He immediately followed this up with a proviso, a condition, that was necessary to guarantee delivery.

> '*If you see me taken from you, it shall be so for you,*
> *but if not, it shall not be so.*'
>
> 2 Kings 2:10 (KJV Modernized)

Why did Elijah say it was '*a hard thing*'? I believe there are three possible reasons Elijah thought this was '*a hard thing*'. Considering what he had been through, Elijah could have been saying, 'You really don't know what you are asking!' Next, Elijah may have been saying, 'It is not mine to give'(f). If this was the nature of his response, Elijah was saying that he wasn't in the place to bestow what was God's right to impart.

Finally, Elijah, like Jesus, could have been saying, '*You are requesting to drink of the cup of affliction, that I have had to drink, and you are requesting to be baptised with the death and separation I have had to endure*' (personalised adaption of (3)). If this is the case, Elijah was communicating the total sacrifice that accompanied the responsibility Elisha sought. Addressing the same need, Jesus addresses James' and John's jockeying for position by saying,

> '*...whoever desires to become great among you, let him be your servant. And whoever desires to be first among you, let him be your slave - just as the Son of Man did not come to be*

(f) In the vein of James' and John's mother, who requested her boys sit either side of Jesus when He came into His kingdom (2). In that situation, Jesus responded by saying,

'*...to sit on My right hand and on My left is not Mine to give, but it is for those for whom it is prepared by My Father,*' Matthew 20:23.

(1) 2 Kings 2:10. (2) Matthew 20:21. (3) Matthew 20:22.

served, but to serve, and to give His life a ransom for many.'

Matthew 20:26-28.

40: Gestation

Was Elisha's apprenticeship 40 months?

1 Samuel 17:16; For 40 days Goliath taunted Israel (stood between Israel and their claim to the Promised Land).

Genesis 7:12; Flood 40 days to a new world.

Numbers 14:34; Israel 40 days - led to 40 years in the wilderness.

Matthew 4:2; Jesus 40 days through wilderness entry.

Was Jesus with his disciples for 40 months?

Acts 1:3; Jesus 40 days with disciples speaking of things pertaining to the kingdom.

The Need to See

I believe it was this knowledge of the cost of true fatherhood that Elijah referred to when he said, '*You have asked a hard thing*', (2 Kings 2:10). He followed that with the condition for the bestowment of the request by saying,

'If you see me taken from you, it shall be so for you, but if not, it shall not be so.'

2 Kings 2:10 (KJV Modernized)

Here we understand that the granting of the request was contingent on '*seeing*'. That is, seeing on the other side of Jordan or, in the spirit realm. If he saw, he had it! He was to see the true armies of Israel - chariots and angel horsemen of fire - carried by the whirlwind of God, which were to separate him from Elijah. Elijah knew that God by His Spirit reveals things in the eternal or unseen realm to those who love Him.

'Eye has not seen, nor ear heard,
Nor have entered into the heart of man
The things which God has prepared for those who love Him.
But God has revealed them to us by His Spirit.'

1 Corinthians 2:9-10

In seeing his master's departure Elisha was literally proven to be one who '*loved unto death*' (1). This is attested to by his gut-wrenching cry, '*My father, my father...*' (2) and in the tearing of his robes (3). As such, he was also confirmed as a completely broken vessel and ready to emanate the glory of God (4). His subsequent picking up of Elijah's mantle paralleled

(1) Revelation 12:11. (2) 2 Kings 2:12. (3) 2 Kings 2:12; Matthew 27:51; Hebrews 10:20. (4) Judges 7:20.

what was taking place in his heart. He had died that God could live through him (1). Like Abraham, he had arrived at his 'Mount Moriah' moment where, '*In the mount of the Lord, it shall be seen*' (2). And like Isaiah, whose hero king was removed so that he could '*see also*' (3), Elisha had his dependence severed and 'saw' (4).

It is one thing to be baptised or initiated into Christ, and quite another to die so that He can live through you. We truly enter the fullness of the kingdom when He lives through us. Elisha was proven to be one of the '*many called*', but who made the journey to be '*chosen*' (5). This was not a forced journey, he could have stopped at a multiple of places along the way, but hope and faith carried him on, until '*loving not his own life unto death*' (6) he was resurrected into fatherhood authority as a walking portal of the kingdom (g).

(g) That Elisha needed an apprenticeship at all and did not simply take on Elijah's mantle the day it was thrown over him, or even pick up the mantle at the end of the day, without undergoing the journey, is a challenge to those who believe Christ's words, '*It is finished!*' mean we have already arrived. This is clearly not the case, when the Apostle Paul, himself, insisted we follow him, as he followed Christ (1 Corinthians 11:1), and that maturity is marked by those undertaking this journey (Philippians 3:8-15).

(1) cf. Colossians 3:3. (2) Genesis 22:14. (3) Isaiah 6:1. (4) 2 Kings 2:12. (5) Matthew 20:16; 22:14. (6) Matthew 20:16; 22:14.

Prayer:

Father, I thank You that just as Elisha crossed Jordan in the shadow of his master, a way has been made for me, with Christ, to enter heaven. I am challenged that the fullness of my destiny will be reached in proportion to my surrender. I openly choose to press in for the prize of standing before You. Let Your love so envelop me that my dependency on this realm will be totally eclipsed by our relationship, and I too be a father to those who follow. Amen.

Summary:

- The mystic journey along the ancient paths is one:

    - of maturing spiritually
    - that develops the eternal virtues: hope, faith and love
    - of ever-increasing personal surrender.

- There are tests along the way that present legitimate reasons to end the journey.

- Bethel speaks of childhood hope.

- If we remain at the place of hope and do not see the promise materialize, we become disillusioned. Disillusioned people become disinterested and disengaged.

- Jericho speaks of living by faith.

- The journey to Jordan is that which distinguishes fathers from sons.

- Jordan is the place of loving others as yourself.

- Along the way we have to silence the voice of unbelief. At Bethel, we are to silence the voice of dependence on the 'seen' realm. At Jericho we are to silence the voice of reason.

- The cost of true fatherhood is why Elijah exclaimed, *'You have asked a hard thing!'*

- The Spirit of God reveals things of the eternal realm to those who love Him.

- We truly enter the fullness of the kingdom when He lives through us.

Chapter 15

The Fear of the Lord

The Burning Ones

The launching point for our final discussion is the first recorded miracle in John's Gospel - the turning of water into wine at the wedding in Cana (1). This scenario tells of water in six stone pots being miraculously turned into wine. The six waterpots are representative of man (a), and in Jesus turning their contents into wine, He is not only working a miracle, but is also performing a deeply symbolic prophetic act. This sign points to His death in three years time. His sacrifice will cleanse believers, so that they may enter into a new level of union with God and be filled with the wine of His Spirit (b, c) This incident closes with the words,

(a) Man was created on the sixth day (Genesis 1: 27, 31), therefore 6 is generally accepted as the number of man/flesh/physical.

(b) The parallel and association of wine and the Spirit of God: Acts 2:4, 15; Ephesians 5:18.

(c) When did the water become wine? When it became an offering! 2 Samuel 23:15-17.

(1) John 2:1-11.

205

'This <u>beginning</u> of miracles did Jesus in Cana of Galilee, and manifested forth his glory; and his disciples believed on him.'

John 2:11 (KJV)

What may surprise you is that I believe this is not the first miracle Jesus performed. I hear you saying, 'What?!' Let me present what the Scriptures say before you make a judgment. In describing the wedding scene, John says, *'And both Jesus was called, and his disciples, to the marriage'* (1). If the disciples were with Him, it is reasonable to assume that Peter is there amongst them. If Peter is there then this is not the first miracle (in chronological terms), because Peter was called after a miracle catch of fish (2). Reinforcing this point is that when Nicodemus meets with Christ he says to Jesus, *'...No one can do these miracles that You do unless God is with him,'* (3). Well, according to John's record there has only been one miracle, thus far, whereas Nicodemus acknowledges that He has performed miracles (plural). Nicodemus is thus making reference to more miracles than turning the water into wine. This explains why Mary would say to the servants, *'Whatever He says to you, do it'* (4). She knows from experience that if you do what Jesus says miracles pop! (d).

(d) Universal truth: Do what He says. True as much today, as it was then.

So, why does John say this is the *'beginning of miracles'*? And, if this is not the first miracle, why does John say that the next miracle is *'the second'* miracle (5)? These are valid questions. In providing an answer we need to recognize that the word *'beginning'* (Greek word, 'arche'), not only means the 'first' chronologically, it also means, 'the commencement of something', 'the head', 'the outer most point', 'rule, power, dominion', and that which has 'priority', or is 'preeminent'. Considering Peter's presence at the wedding, Nicodemus' reference to plural miracles and Jesus' mother's comments, may I suggest that John is not merely referencing this miracle

(1) John 2:2. (2) Luke 5:6, 8-11. (3) John 3:2. (4) John 2:5. (5) John 4:54.

as the first chronologically.

John's Gospel, which as we have seen is deeply mystical in nature, records Jesus performing seven miracles or signs. John is not merely filling in what was missed in the Synoptic Gospels (e), he has deliberately chosen these particular signs to relate a deeper truth. I suggest that the healing of the nobleman's son, the '*second sign*' (1), is described as such so that the corporate sequence which is revealed is greater than each individual sign. It is important that we take an overview of the seven miracle signs to appreciate why John denotes the miracle at the wedding, as the '*beginning*'. The seven signs are:

1. Water turned to wine (John 2:1-11)
2. Healing of the nobleman's son (John 4:46-54)
3. Healing of the lame man at the pool of Bethesda (John 5:1-15)
4. The feeding of the 5000 (John 6:1-13)
5. Walking on the water (John 6:15-21)
6. Opening the eyes of the blind man (John 9:1-7)
7. The resurrection of Lazarus (John 11:1-44)

After reading the chapter on Hebrew poetry I hope you can see that the seven signs form a chiasm (X), with the centrepiece being the feeding of the 5000. May I also suggest that the use of the word '*beginning*' for the miracle at the wedding at Cana has more to do with its content than it has with chronology. That's because John, the Apostle of love, is speaking in terms better understood from an Eastern viewpoint, than a Western mindset. Repeatedly, throughout the Bible's poetic writings, the word '*beginning*' is used in association with one particular facet of;

'*The fear of the Lord is the <u>beginning</u> of wisdom....*'

Psalm 111:10 (Emphasis added)

'*The fear of the Lord is the <u>beginning</u> of knowledge,*

(e) Signs in John compared with the synoptic gospels

- water to wine (John)

- healing of nobleman's son (Matthew 8:5-13; Luke 7:1-10)

- man at pool of Bethesda (John)

- feed 5000 (Matthew 14:13-21; Mark 6:30-44; Luke 9:10-17)

- walking on water (Matthew 14:22-33; Mark 6:45-52)

- healing of man born blind (John)

- Lazarus' resurrection (John)

(1) John 4:54.

> *But fools despise wisdom and instruction.'*
>
> Proverbs 1:7 (Emphasis added)

> *'The fear of the Lord is the <u>beginning</u> of wisdom,*
> *And the knowledge of the Holy One is understanding.'*
>
> Proverbs 9:10 (Emphasis added)

A Western mindset will think that these three verses are contradictory because two of them say the fear of the Lord leads to wisdom while the other says it leads to knowledge. The Bible teaches that wisdom leads to understanding which in turn leads to knowledge (1), so that wisdom is like a point of call on the road to knowledge. Therefore, the fear of the Lord is the beginning of both wisdom and knowledge at the same time. That said, the word, *'beginning'* is a marker to point us to *'the fear of the Lord'*. John is not speaking chronologically about the signs, he is speaking on a deeper level about something that commences with *'the fear of the Lord'*. The seven signs point to something with more spiritual significance than seven individual miracles.

This seven-fold (seven signs) outbreaking confirms Christ as the Messiah. The seven-fold Spirit of God, as described by Isaiah, puts this truth in focus.

(f) Be aware there are almost as many interpretations of the Seven Spirits of God and their associated texts as there are teachers of the word. This interpretation is presented for consideration from my understanding at the time of writing.

> *'And there shall come forth a rod out of the stem of Jesse, and a Branch shall grow out of his roots: And the spirit of the Lord shall rest upon him, the spirit of wisdom and understanding, the spirit of counsel and might, the spirit of knowledge and of the fear of the Lord.'*
>
> Isaiah 11:1-2 (KJV)

What Isaiah and John are both presenting to us is the seven-fold Spirit of God pictured as the Menorah (f). Notice

(1) Proverbs 3:19-20, 14:6, 24:3-4.

the couplets - wisdom and understanding, counsel and might, knowledge and fear of the Lord - as the twin side branches of the Menorah, while the Spirit of the Lord stands alone as the central stem. In this way, John's signs/miracles look like this,

Water turned to wine - Spirit of the Fear of the Lord
Healing of the nobleman's son - Spirit of Wisdom
Healing the lame man, the pool of Bethesda - Spirit of Counsel
The feeding of the 5000 - Spirit of the Lord
Walking on the water - Spirit of Might
Opening the eyes of the blind man - Spirit of Understanding
The resurrection of Lazarus - Spirit of Knowledge

This is reinforced by understanding that it is only when the individual lamps (g) are combined that they reveal the luminary or light (h). John said it like this,

'This beginning of miracles did Jesus in Cana of Galilee, and manifested forth his glory; and his disciples believed on him.'

John 2:11 (KJV)

(g) Lamp: Niyr (H5214) of the Menorah, which in Hebrew literally means, 'the breaking of the untilled ground'.

(h) Light: Maor (H3974) meaning luminary, a light.

Each of the seven miracles display Jesus operating in each of the seven Spirits of God. They are an outbreaking from His being that confirm Him as being both the Door of Eternity, and as carrying the Eternal Light or Glory of God. We can now focus on *'the Spirit of the fear of the Lord'* as the prerequisite of the glory.

The fear of the Lord is a facet of worship not well understood in Western minds. At best, westerners equate the fear of the Lord with reverence and awe of God, which falls well short of its meaning. However, before venturing into what is meant by the term let's confirm its relevance to us as New Testament believers by highlighting a few verses.

'Having therefore these promises, dearly beloved, let us cleanse ourselves from all filthiness of the flesh and spirit, perfecting holiness in <u>the fear of God</u>.'

2 Corinthians 7:1 (KJV, Emphasis added)

And,

'Submitting yourselves one to another in <u>the fear of God</u>.'

Ephesians 5:21 (KJV, Emphasis added)

And,

*'Therefore as we are receiving a kingdom which cannot be shaken, let us have grace,
whereby we may serve God acceptably with reverence
and <u>godly fear</u>.'*

Hebrews 12:28 (KJV, Emphasis added)

These verses declare that not only is *'the fear of the Lord'*, or as the New Testament has it *'the fear of God'*, a timeless facet of the worship of God, but they show it to be the foundation for maturing. The fear of the Lord is the basis for true submission and partners with grace for service in the kingdom. Our lack of understanding of the term only emphasises the importance of getting a solid hold on the subject. Its relevance to mystics entering the eternal realm of the kingdom is even greater because the poetic authors within scripture declare it to be, above all else, the key into the glory. The verse quoted earlier, *'The fear of the Lord is the beginning of knowledge...'* (1), declares that an active fear of the Lord leads to the experiential knowledge of God. This is confirmed by David when he writes,

*'The secret of the Lord is with those who fear Him;
and He will show them His covenant'*

Psalm 25:14

(1) Proverbs 1:7.

The '*secret*' is that which is shared in intimate confidentiality with the closest of friends. That which is shared are the appropriate promises of His covenant that fit our individual situations. The fruit of this intimacy with God, which requires a right spirit coupled with an active fear of the Lord, is refined by the writer of proverbs, who says,

> '*By humility and the fear of the Lord are riches,*
> *and honor, and life.*'

> Proverbs 22:4

God declares He will provide the means to gain wealth, carry the glory and be a conduit for the Life of God to the person entering at this level (i). This last point is reiterated by,

> '*The fear of the Lord is a fountain of life....*'

> Proverbs 14:27

In the light of Jesus' teaching about the Spirit flowing out of the heart (1), this verse suggests that the fear of the Lord is a heart issue. It is a metaphor for us to picture our hearts as that portal through which heaven flows. It also advances the idea that the fear of the Lord opens the gate into that realm. Much more is written about the benefits of the fear of the Lord (j), but we need to move on to better understand the term and unlock its provision.

Thinking of the fear of the Lord simply as a reverence and awe of God falls well short of its true meaning because it does not necessarily ensure heart participation. Nor does it tell us how the term was conceived or enable us to grasp the depth of application it carries. King David takes us part of the way when he writes,

> '*Come, you children, listen to me; I will teach you the fear*

(i) Riches: oser (H6239), a noun used in reference to wealth, riches. It describes various kinds of wealth in land, possessions, cattle, and descendants.

Honor:kabod (H3519), a masculine singular noun referring to honor, glory, majesty, wealth.

Life: hay (H2417), an Aramaic adjective meaning living, alive.

(j) See next page.

(1) John 7:39.

(j) Benefits of the fear of the Lord Protection, long life, riches, wisdom, knowledge, secrets, blessed.

- Job 1:8-10 hedge of protection
- Job 28:28 wisdom
- Psalm 25:12 teach His way
- Psalm 33:18 watched over by God
- Psalm 34:7 angelic protection
- Psalm 34:9 no want
- Psalm 86:11 united heart
- Psalm 103:17 everlasting mercy
- Psalm 111:10 beginning of wisdom
- Psalm 112:1; 115:13; 128:1, 4; blessed
- Psalm 115:11 help and shield
- Psalm 147:11 God takes pleasure in
- Proverbs 1:7 beginning of knowledge
- Proverbs 2:5 find the knowledge of God
- Proverbs 9:10 beginning of wisdom
- Proverbs 10:27 prolongs life
- Proverbs 14:26 strong confidence, children place of refuge
- Proverbs 14:27 fountain of life
- Proverbs 15:33 instruction of wisdom
- Proverbs 19:23 tends to life
- Proverbs 22:4 riches, honor, and life (coupled with humility)
- Proverbs 23:17 day long activity
- Proverbs 29:25 opposite to fear of man.

(k) This is why Namaan, the leper who was healed under the ministry of Elisha, requests that he be able to take with him back to Syria two mule loads of earth, that he may be able to worship the God of Israel (2 Kings 5:17).

of the Lord. Who is the man who desires life, and loves many days, that he may see good? Keep your tongue from evil, and your lips from speaking deceit.'

Psalm 34:11-13

David reveals that the fear of the Lord is the key to a long life (1). He ties that longevity to the power of our own words. In doing so he says that a person with the fear of the Lord has an understanding of the reverence and awe of God to the point that it not only influences what he does, it also affects the last vestige of human surrender, the tongue and what is spoken (2). Selah.

To fully plumb the depth of the fear of the Lord we need to go back to the time of the Patriarchs - Abraham, Isaac and Jacob. As travellers in the Promised Land their *'fear'* of God was displayed and activated by sacrifice upon an altar. They did this because in the Middle East there was a perceived association between gods and the land (k). When Abraham nomadically moves about the land he offers sacrifice upon an altar in each location to invoke God's blessing and protection (3). The climax of Abraham's spiritual journey takes place at the altar on Mount Moriah, where he offers up his son (the Akedah) (4). By putting his future on the line in offering up Isaac, the love of his life, God responded by saying,

'Do not lay your hand on the lad, or do anything to him: for <u>now I know that you fear God</u>, since you have not withheld your son, your only son from Me.'

Genesis 22:12

(1) Psalm 33:18-19; Proverbs 10:27, 19:23, 22:4. (2) Psalm 12:4; Matthew 12:34; James 3:1-12 cf. Romans 3:13-18. (3) Genesis 12:7, 8; 13:4; 15:1, 7-18; cf. Genesis 26:24-25. (4) Genesis 22:1-19.

Such is the impact of this event, that later reference to the God of Abraham, Isaac and Jacob includes *'the fear of Isaac'* (1). Clearly, this marks Isaac's willingness to participate in being offered up to God. Check it out; reread the Akedah in scripture and see if there is any hint of a struggle between father and son (2). There is none.

Further to this, it is stated that Abraham *'saddled his ass'* (3). The saddling of an ass is a servant's duty and Abraham had servants who were going to make the journey with him (4). In recording that Abraham performed this duty, the Lord is telling us that Abraham is not merely outwardly saddling his donkey, he is also *'saddling'* his heart in obedience as a servant of God. Abraham repeats (l) *'Here I am'* (5) throughout the episode, which clearly marks his servant attitude.

After Abraham laid the wood on his son he took the fire for the sacrifice in his hand (6). Again, we are looking at a deeply significant act. The fire in his hand is a depiction of the fire of sacrifice already burning in his heart (m).

As a consequence of Abraham's sacrificial obedience, God released the following promise over him.

> *'Blessing I will bless you, and multiplying I will multiply your descendants as the stars of heaven and as the sand which is on the seashore; and your descendants shall possess the gate of their enemies.'*

> Genesis 22:17

It is a true interpretation that Abraham was blessed to be a blessing and that his physical offspring would become numerous and overcome their foes. However, it has application on at least two more levels. The word, *'bless'* and *'blessing'* is the Hebrew word, 'barak' which refers to the bending of the knee in humble

(l) Refrain: a recurring phrase or chorus line throughout a song or poem. ie. Psalm 136.

(m) See section on the Hebrew letter, 'Kaph' under 'Joshua's carbon footprint' in chapter 3.

Note also the association between heart and hand in these verses: Exodus 35:25; Deuteronomy 8:17; 11:18; 15:7; Judges 7: 20; James 4:8.

(1) Genesis 31:42, 53. (2) Genesis 22:1-19. (3) Genesis 22:3. (4) Genesis 22:3. (5) Genesis 22:1, 7, 11. (6) Genesis 22:6.

obedience to receive a blessing and suggests the impartation from a higher to a lower. The word, *'multiplying'* and *'multiply'* is the Hebrew word, 'rabah', which means 'much, many and abundant'. Given that Abraham has just put action to his faith by offering up his son, the promise made by God has a deeper significance than appears in English. A paraphrase of what God said would be something like, *'In your humble obedience I will bestow from heaven, and in giving your all I will release heaven's storehouse through you'*. Because the word, *'descendants'* is the Hebrew word 'zera', which actually means 'seed' (n), there are also two layers of fruit being released here. There is the seed of offspring and descendants and there is the seed of the word. Abraham's *'fear of God'* was manifest in humbly offering his all. The promise that act invoked was his hearing (seed) from heaven (stars) that would manifest on earth (sand). Effectively, God's word to him became flesh. This was true of Jesus, not just in His coming, but also in His ministry, and it is true for us as we enter the same level of consecration.

Against this historical backdrop may I suggest that the fear of the Lord is so much more than reverence and awe for God. It would be better expressed as reverence and awe for God put into action, which is a totally different matter.

What does it look like? It looks like an Isaac. It is a life presented on the altar of our hearts, totally surrendered to God in obedient servanthood. It recognizes the creative power of the spoken word and, as such, it looks like a David or a Samson level of consecration, ensuring that only what is holy passes across the lips (1). And it looks like Jesus in becoming a channel for the timeless reality of heaven, offering up His life, turning the water of the Word of God into the blood of sacrifice (water to wine (2) (o)), and becoming a portal for heaven to break out on earth. Its benefits cannot be measured. It is the access code to heaven's storehouse.

(n) Seed in scripture:

Offspring: Genesis 3:15, 4:25, 9:9, 12:7; 13:15.

Words:

Matthew 13:9 ff;

Luke 8:11.

Promise/s: Galatians 3:19; Hebrews 11:11.

Potential: John 12:24; Matthew 13:23.

Fruitfulness: Genesis 1:11, 29.

(o) Water and blood can also speak of words backed up with the sacrifice of His life.

(1) Judges 13:7; Psalm 34:13. (2) John 2:7-10; cf. 1 John 5:6.

Though we may traditionally picture the 'burning ones' as those on fire for God in the sense of being zealous to do His will, the reality is that the true burning ones are living sacrifices. They are those who have tasted the eternal realm and yielded their lives to be full of the Spirit of the fear of the Lord. Nothing less than all that God has will satisfy them. They no longer live for themselves, but have separated themselves from the world and unto Him that they may inherit a greater kingdom. There is not just the water of words, but the blood of their lives on offer so that heaven may manifest on earth and God be glorified through them. The true mystics are those who enter in to hear the Master's voice and do it. They are the grain of wheat fallen to the ground to bring heaven's multiplication through them (1); those who have lost their lives to find them (2); those who have been crucified with Christ that He may live in them (3). And He beckons us, the church, to join them.

Prayer:

Father, I am undone. I consecrate myself to You that You would fill me with the Spirit of the fear of the Lord. Please forgive me for my independent heart and the looseness of my lips. Remind me to guard my heart and mouth so that what flows through may be used to create, edify and heal. I desire with all my heart to fellowship with You so that I may hear your voice and, as a servant, do what You ask of me. Let a new level of oneness with You mark my life so that heaven may break forth through me, that others encounter You and glorify Your name. Amen.

(1) John 12:24. (2) Matthew 10:39. (3) Galatians 2:20.

Summary:

- The turning of the water into wine is not the first miracle (chronologically), because:

  - the disciples are with Jesus at the wedding and Peter was called by a miracle catch of fish.
  - Nicodemus refers to miracles (plural), and according to John there has only been one miracle.
  - Jesus' mother commands the servants to do what He says from experience.

- If we do what Jesus says the eternal realm breaks through into this world.

- As some of John's signs are in the synoptics and some not, John is choosing his signs to reveal a deeper truth.

- The word '*beginning*' has more to do with the sign's content rather than its chronology.

- The '*beginning*' of signs marks a display of the Fear of the Lord.

- The seven signs of John's gospel confirm Christ as the Messiah, as identified by the seven-fold Spirit of God (Isaiah 11:2), pictured as the Menorah.

- The Fear of the Lord is more than a reverence and awe of God.

- The Fear of the Lord is relevant to New Testament believers.

- David reveals that a true Fear of the Lord affects the tongue as the last vestige of human surrender.

- Abraham's action in offering up his son at Mount Moriah is the ultimate display of the Fear of the Lord.

- A true Fear of the Lord is a laying down of one's life and future in obedience to God.

- Operating in the Fear of the Lord sees heaven manifest on earth.

- The Fear of the Lord is reverence and awe of God put into action.

- The true burning ones are not merely those zealous for God, but living sacrifices.

- The water of their words is backed by the blood of their life (in those that fear God).

The Mystic Awakening

Subject Landscape & Chapter Milestones $\frac{5}{5}$

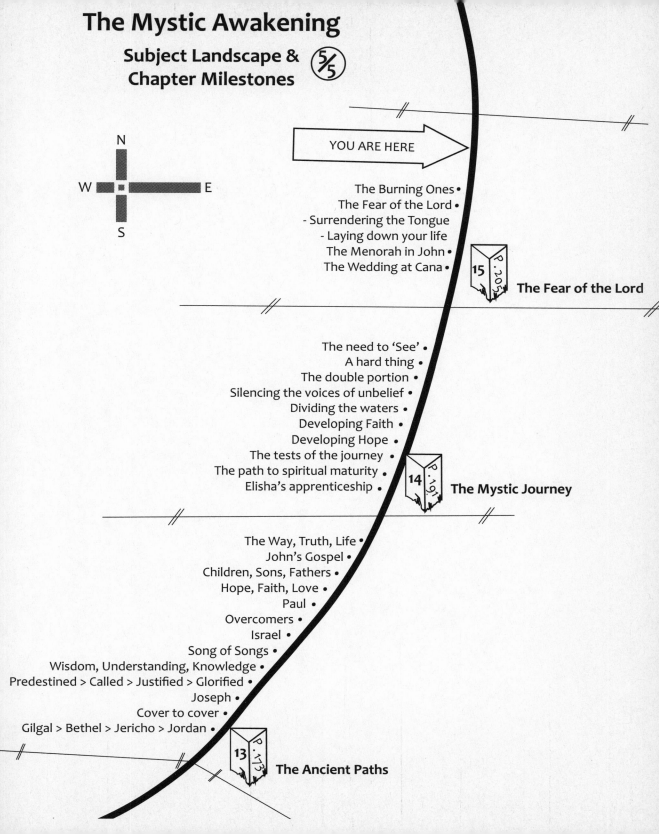

N
W   E
S

YOU ARE HERE

The Burning Ones •
The Fear of the Lord •
- Surrendering the Tongue
- Laying down your life
The Menorah in John •
The Wedding at Cana •

15   P. 205

The Fear of the Lord

The need to 'See' •
A hard thing •
The double portion •
Silencing the voices of unbelief •
Dividing the waters •
Developing Faith •
Developing Hope •
The tests of the journey •
The path to spiritual maturity •
Elisha's apprenticeship •

14   P. 191

The Mystic Journey

The Way, Truth, Life •
John's Gospel •
Children, Sons, Fathers •
Hope, Faith, Love •
Paul •
Overcomers •
Israel •
Song of Songs •
Wisdom, Understanding, Knowledge •
Predestined > Called > Justified > Glorified •
Joseph •
Cover to cover •
Gilgal > Bethel > Jericho > Jordan •

13   P. 173

The Ancient Paths

Subject Index

FREE E-BOOKS?
YES, PLEASE!

Get **FREE** and deeply-discounted **Christian books** for your **e-reader** delivered to your inbox **every week!**

IT'S SIMPLE!

VISIT lovetoreadclub.com

SUBSCRIBE by entering your email address

RECEIVE free and discounted e-book offers and inspiring articles delivered to your inbox every week!

Unsubscribe at any time.

SUBSCRIBE NOW!

LOVE TO READ CLUB

visit **LOVETOREADCLUB.COM** ▶